CONFLICT OF INTERESTS

CONFLICT OF INTERESTS

The Politics of American Education

Joel Spring
University of Cincinnati

Longman
New York & London

Conflict of Interests

Longman Inc., 95 Church Street, White Plains, N. Y. 10601

Associated companies:
Longman Group Ltd., London
Longman Cheshire Pty., Melbourne
Longman Paul Pty., Auckland
Copp Clark Pitman, Toronto
Pitman Publishing Inc., New York

Executive editor: Raymond T. O'Connell
Production editor: Helen B. Ambrosio
Text design: Joseph DePinho
Cover design and sculpture: Joseph DePinho
Cover photo: PhotoGraphic Images
Production supervisor: Judith Stern

Library of Congress Cataloging in Publication Data
Spring, Joel H.
  Conflict of interests.

  Bibliography: p.
  Includes index.
  1. Education and state—United States. 2. Politics
and education—United States. I. Title.
LC89.S66 1988   379.73   87-17300
ISBN 0-582-28677-8

Compositor: Graphicraft Typesetters Ltd.
Printer: Malloy Lithographing, Inc.

  89 90 91 92 93 9 8 7 6 5 4 3

Contents

CONFLICT OF INTERESTS

CHAPTER 1

The Political Structure of American Education

The politics of education in the United States involves a complex interrelationship among government administrators, interest groups, politicians, and knowledge brokers. The educational system is given dynamic force by each group's pursuit of a particular set of educational interests. A major result of this dynamic force is an educational system in a constant state of change.

This chapter presents a broad picture of the educational system. Several themes integrate the various elements of the portrait. One theme is the role of self-interest. Politics involves the pursuit of power and control, and each actor in the drama is motivated by self-interest. In education, self-interest involves complex concerns about personal gain and achievement, beliefs about correct educational practices, and the desire to protect students and institutions.

SELF-INTEREST AND EDUCATIONAL IDEOLOGIES

Across the whole educational structure, individuals and groups want schools to serve particular goals and needs. For instance, teachers' unions want higher salaries and a workplace organized to enhance their professional autonomy. Corporations want the schools to be economically efficient and to produce well-trained workers. Politicians use educational issues to win votes.

In none of the preceding examples is self-interest pursued purely for crass economic gain. In American life, education is a religion of hope for creating a better life. People believe in the power of the schools to do good. A politician can use educational issues to gain votes—for example, promising to expand vocational education as a means of improving the economy—and, at the same time, believe in the beneficial power of vocational training. Teachers' unions can pursue policies that enhance the status and income of their members, and also believe that those policies will improve the schools and education. Most educational proposals arise from a belief that the end result will be the betterment of society.

Therefore, a discussion of the role of self-interest in education requires a description of *educational ideologies*. Ideologies justify methods for controlling educational institutions and educational practices. Various ideologies promote different principles of psychology, interpretations of history, economic and political theories, methods of instruction, and organizational theories. In other words, different sets of ideas support different political interests. For instance, teachers and their unions find more support for professional autonomy in psychological theories that advocate individual decision making than they do in behavioral theories that advocate the control of teacher behavior through management by objectives. In the latter case, recent theories in cognitive psychology portray the teacher as an autonomous thinker making choices about instruction in the context of a constantly changing classroom. In the former case of behavioral psychology, the teacher is considered as a complex set of behaviors that need to be guided and modified by objectives that are written in purely behavioral outcomes. On the other hand, school administrators find their professional positions enhanced by management by objectives.

While ideologies and self-interest link the complex relationships in the politics of American education, the concept of change explains its dynamic qualities. In the twentieth century, the policies, organization, and methods of instruction in American schools have been in constant flux. In part, this is a result of the conflicts of interest that occur in educational politics. In addition, built into the structure of American education is a constant tendency to change. For instance, at the federal level, educational policy changes with every change of national administration; and at the local level, school administrators build their careers on doing something new. Therefore, change is a product of the political tensions in the system and is inherent in the structure.

Self-interest, ideology, and continual change add to the complexity of an educational system that has many layers of governance. Historically, state governments have turned most governing powers over to local boards of education. In recent years, the federal government has emerged as an important determiner of national educational policy. In addition, state governments have assumed greater control of local educational systems. The actions of these three layers of educational government are also influenced by court decisions. At each level of government, interest groups compete for influence, and the knowledge industry seeks economic gains.

The primary purpose of this book is to explain how this complex political system produces educational policy. In this explanation, the word "politics" will refer to the pursuit of power and control over the educational system. This chapter gives a general outline of the power relationships in the organization of American education.

In a broader context, the term "politics of education" refers to the struggle to control the educational system in order to gain power over the general political system and other social organizations. Chapter 2 will discuss how the educational system is used to serve political ends.

Following the presentation of this general framework for interpreting educational politics, there will be a discussion of the political activities of each layer of government, the courts, and the knowledge industry. Included in these chapters will be suggestions on how to analyze political events in education and how to work effectively within the system. The book will conclude with a discussion of political theory and education.

MAJOR POLITICAL ACTORS

For the purposes of analysis, the political system in education can be divided into major government actors, special-interest groups, and the knowledge industry. Within each of these categories, individuals and organizations pursue a particular set of interests and goals. In Table 1.1, these categories are divided into their various parts.

TABLE 1.1 THE MAJOR POLITICAL GROUPS IN EDUCATION

Major Government Actors	Special-Interest Groups	The Knowledge Industry
Politicians	The Big Three	Creators
Educational politicians	Foundations	Funding agencies
School boards	Corporate Sector	Researchers
Courts	Teachers' unions	Gatekeepers
	Educational interest groups	Knowledge brokers
	Single-interest groups	Testing organizations
		Distributors
		Publishing industry

Let us consider the major government actors, which include elected politicians, educational politicians, school boards, and the courts. These groups, in varying degrees, have particular educational interests that foster continual dynamic change.

Because they are concerned with maintaining voter support, politicians must please their constituencies. Often, they must please particular educational constituencies. For instance, in the 1980s well-defined educational constituencies emerged within each national political party. The Democratic party, in most cases, had the support of the most powerful educational interest groups, the two teachers' unions. The Republican party, under the leadership of Ronald Reagan, built an educational coalition that consisted of private-school groups, religious organizations that were critical of the moral values taught in the public schools, conservative school reformers, and advocates of school prayer.

With such well-defined educational constituencies, presidential candidates of each party must now formulate, if they are to retain voter support, educational policies that will please their educational backers. In practice, this means that each new president must offer a new set of educational policies. This situation keeps national educational policy in a constant state of flux.

Members of Congress sometimes feel a tension between the educational policies of their party and the desires of the voters in their particular state or congressional district. For instance, Ronald Reagan never won full support from Republican members of Congress for his proposals to abolish the Department of Education, create tuition tax credits, and allow school prayer. Members of Congress often feel political pressure from special-interest groups in their state or district. The two teachers' unions are well organized and place a great deal of pressure on local politicians. Such local pressure can force a member of Congress to reject the policies of his or her political party.[1]

Some politicians in Congress attempt to build their careers on educational issues. For instance, in return for support from the two teachers' unions, a member of Congress might agree to support union-approved legislation. In return, the unions might supply him or her with campaign funds and aid. Support from educational organizations can be very important in a political campaign; they can help out with door-to-door campaigning, issue letters of support, and provide volunteers. In other situations, a member of Congress might have a strong special-interest group in her or his district that supports school prayer or bilingual education.[2]

Politicans at the state level are vulnerable to special-interest groups. In the 1980s, many state governors jumped on the educational bandwagon, claiming that school reforms would revitalize their states' economies. In part, they felt pressure from corporations to produce better-educated workers for the labor market. Like national educa tional policy, a state's educational policy will change to meet political goals.

Members of state legislatures experience pressure from several sources. Some are contacted directly by local school superintendents and school boards. Others are pressured by state teachers' organiza- tions and other educational groups. In recent years, many members of state legislatures have become experts in school finance policies.[3] This has left them open to pressures from taxpayers' groups and corporations.

Educational Politicians

Working at the behest of elected politicians are the *educational politicians*. These are educational administrators whose tenure de- pends on the favor of elected politicians or on voter support. At the federal level, examples would include the secretary of education and assistant secretaries, and at the state level, state superintendents of education. Some state superintendents are appointed and others are elected. In most local districts, superintendents are appointed by local school boards and depend on their continued support.

Educational politicians retain their positions by serving the interests of those responsible for putting them in office. This does not mean educational politicians lack ideals or are pawns of the powerful. In most cases, educational politicians share the same ideological outlook as the interests they serve.

At the federal level, the secretary of education serves the adminis- tration and can be caught in political crossfire. The Department of Education and the position of secretary of education were created in the late 1970s during the Carter administration. Before then, the administrative branch was headed by a commissioner of education in the Department of Health, Education, and Welfare. During the 1976 presidential campaign, Jimmy Carter promised the National Educa- tion Association (NEA), the largest of the two teachers' unions, to establish a department of education in return for support and cam- paign aid. The primary responsibility of the secretary of education is to represent the administration's viewpoint on educational matters before Congress and the public. In addition, the Department of Educa- tion administers educational legislation passed by Congress and prepares legislation designed to carry out the administration's educa- tional objectives. The task of administering educational legislation involves a range of activities: from supporting research and collecting statistics to regulating educational programs.

A variety of political forces create difficulties for educational politicians. After he left office, Terrel Bell, secretary of education in the Reagan administration, complained of constant pressure from what he called the "radical right" of the Republican party. Bell wrote about his experience, "Among the members of the radical right, the thinking was that I and others like me were keeping Reagan from being Reagan." While in office, Bell campaigned for the conservative educational agenda of the Reagan administration, which included changing academic standards for graduation from high school and for teacher education. He resisted pressure from the radical right to enact the more conservative part of the Reagan agenda, which included abolishing the Department of Education, infusing Christian morality into the schools, and expunging secular humanism from the curriculum. In other words, Bell represented the moderate part of the educational coalition brought together by the Reagan campaign.[4]

Bureaucratic Politics

Educational politicians operate in the climate set by their political supporters and within the context of what can be called the *politics of bureaucracy*. At the heart of bureaucratic politics is the pursuit of self-interest by individual bureaucrats. For instance, Terrel Bell admitted that fulfilling the Reagan administration pledge to abolish the Department of Education would mean the abolition of his own position. As Bell wrote, "In working to dissolve the Department of Education, I was unwittingly advocating the destruction of the indispensable power base that I came to realize was necessary for my survival in office." Consequently, Bell decided to make this a low priority on his agenda.[5]

The loyalty of educational politicians is divided between their organization and their political support. In fact, divided loyalties are what distinguish educational politicians from educational bureaucrats. The bureaucrat is loyal primarily to the organization, whereas the educational politician must perform a balancing act between the needs of the bureaucracy and the demands of his or her political supporters.

In most situations educational politicians are interested in maintaining high salaries and expanding the number of jobs within the organization. Certainly, part of their power and prestige depends on the size and wealth of the organization under their command. On the other hand, there are situations in which political policy runs counter to bureaucratic self-interest. Under Terrel Bell, the Department of Education was threatened by President Reagan's desire to reduce spending and abolish the organization. Bureaucrats within the department resisted the budget cuts, while Bell, resisting attempts to do away with the department, was forced to agree to reduced spending.[6]

Promotion from within the organization is primarily a concern of bureaucrats interested in protecting their own occupational mobility. In some cases, educational politicians must resist this bureaucratic tendency so that they can bring in their own people. On the other hand, educational politicians do try to protect their organizations from outside interests and maintain their prestige. As Bell described the situation, he strongly resisted the attacks by the radical right within the Republican party. Obviously, the prestige of educational politicians depends on the prestige of their organizations.

State and Local Politicians

At the state level, educational politicians owe their political loyalty to voters, to governors, or to state boards of education. In almost half the states, school superintendents are elected by popular vote, while in approximately half of the other states they are appointed by state boards of education. In four states they are appointed by governors. Like the secretary of education, they must achieve a balance between loyalty to their political supporters and loyalty to their organizations.

Bill Honig, superintendent of the California school system in the early 1980s, succeeded in building a coalition between widely different groups. To the educational establishment, he promised to support increased educational spending. To minority groups, he promised to raise educational standards in order to improve the quality of the schools. To the business community, he promised better economic performance by raising the quality of high school graduates. In addition, he established contacts with local parent and civic organizations. Once elected to office, he worked to fulfill his pledges to these groups and to maintain harmony in the state educational bureaucracy.[7]

At the local level, most superintendents are appointed by boards of education. Here a distinction must be made between place-oriented and career-oriented school superintendents. A *place-oriented superintendent* plans to remain with a particular school district for a long time. Consequently, the primary political concern of such a superintendent is to win the continued support of the board of education and the local power structure. On the other hand, a *career-oriented superintendent* is interested in serving in the school system that offers the most prestige and money. He or she is interested primarily in building a reputation in national administrative organizations. In both situations, the superintendent must balance political interests against the need to cooperate with the local educational bureaucracy.[8]

The political concern of place-oriented superintendent is to maintain the support of the board of education and the local power structure. Historically, public schools have been controlled by local boards of education, but in recent years more and more of them have fallen under the control of state and federal governments. Most boards of education in the United States are elected in at-large and nonpartisan elections. For reasons that will be discussed in more detail in later chapters, nonpartisan elections tend to be won by members of the business and professional communities. In fact, the typical school board member in the United States is a white male who earns between $40,000 and $50,000 a year and is engaged in a business or a professional occupation. Very often, a local power elite controls school board elections.[9]

To assure her or his place in the school system, the place-oriented superintendent will often join local business-service organizations such as the Chamber of Commerce, Kiwanis Club, Rotary Club, or Lions Club. This provides ready contact with local community leaders who are often connected informally to board of education members and, in some cases, are themselves members of the local board of education. The place-oriented superintendent makes additional informal contacts through church organizations and other community activities.[10]

Like the place-oriented superintendent, the career-oriented superintendent must maintain the same support from the board of education and local community elites, but his or her primary concern is to do something new in the school system that will be recognized by other school boards and administrators across the nation. Consequently, the career-oriented superintendent is constantly driven by the need to institute some form of educational change in the local school district. Sometimes other local administrators, who also must prove their worth by doing something new, join in the effort to institute educational change.

The Court System

The final major government actor in education is the court system. Often, the court system is involved in educational decisions because of a failure in some other part of the political structure. For instance, the black community struggled for many years to end segregated education. Because of limited access to the ballot box and the control exercised by local white elites over boards of education, the black community had to seek redress outside the normal channels of political power. In this case, the black community turned to the court system, which forced state and local power structures to integrate the public schools. In some situations, the courts actually took over local school systems to assure desegregation.[11]

Other groups without political power have followed the same political path. For example, the Chinese community in San Francisco turned to the courts when it was unable to receive special help for Chinese-speaking students, and parents of handicapped children fought in the courts to gain educational attention from local school systems.[12]

In turn, political activity pursued through the courts has produced state and federal laws. Court decisions regarding desegregation, language issues, and the handicapped were all followed by major legislation.[13] Court decisions change local practices while increasing the political power of the related interest groups.

The courts, furthermore, are themselves political institutions. Whether elected or appointed, judges still represent the judicial philosophy of their supporters. United States Supreme Court appointments usually reflect the legal attitudes of the administration in power. As a result of the appointments made by presidents Nixon and Reagan, the Supreme Court in the 1970s and 1980s became more conservative than it had been in the 1950s and 1960s. As later chapters will show, this resulted in major changes in the application of federal laws.

Political pressure exercised through the courts has also changed educational practices. An important example is the school desegregation laws, which led to years of turmoil in the nation's school systems. Of special importance was the use of *magnet schools* in the 1970s as a means of voluntary desegregation. The establishment of magnet schools with special programs to attract students of different races splintered the public school curriculum. Across the nation, separate schools were established for creative and performing arts, special academic programs, and vocational education.

Courts, general politicians, educational politicians, and boards of education exist in a world of constant educational change. In part, such change is the result of efforts to gain and maintain power and of shifting political administrations. Change is also inherent in the very system of governance. Moreover, the pursuit of power and change is justified by educational ideologies. As the knowledge industry creates the ideology, special-interest groups add energy and conflict to the system.

SPECIAL-INTEREST GROUPS

Much of the U.S. political system is based on a symbiotic relationship between special-interest groups, politicians, and government administrators.[14] In this symbiotic relationship, a special-interest group will form around a particular administrative branch of government. For instance, the tobacco lobby has a major interest in continuing subsidies to its industry and works closely with the branch of the Department of Agriculture responsible for the program. In turn, the administrators of the tobacco program depend for their very jobs on the continuation of the subsidy. Therefore, the tobacco lobby and government administrators work together to insure continued congressional funding of the program. In addition, politicians from tobacco-growing areas depend on support from the tobacco lobby. The result is an alliance in which all members depend for their survival on the continuation of a particular government program.

David Stockman, the budget-cutting head of the Office of Management and Budget under President Reagan, has complained that these symbiotic relationships make it impossible to bring about significant changes in the U.S. government. For instance, while Stockman was working to cut the government budget, Senator Jesse Helms of North Carolina, who received strong support from the tobacco lobby, told him in reference to budget cuts, "Now you go right to it, boy. But don't let them OMB bureaucrats down there confuse you. The tobacco program doesn't cost the taxpayers one red cent. And it never will as long as I'm chairman of the Agricultural Committee."[15]

In education, the relationship between special-interest groups and government is more complicated than the one in the preceding example. This complexity is illustrated by the 1986 report of the Carnegie Task Force on Teaching as a Profession, *A Nation Prepared: Teachers for the 21st Century*.[16] The task force included representatives from the three major interest groups: the corporate sector, foundations, and teachers' unions (see Table 1.1).

An important feature of the Carnegie report is its attempt to influence state and local educational policies. The sponsoring foundation, the Carnegie Corporation of New York, used a twofold strategy. First, by organizing and supporting a prestigious panel and paying for the distribution of its report, the foundation hoped to influence thinking about educational policy. Second, by including a political strategy in its report, the foundation hoped to alter educational practices by changing government policy. Such a strategy, backed by foundation funding can exert a powerful influence on U.S. educational practices.

Typically, foundations exercise influence by supporting the creation and dissemination of knowledge. They do this by funding research, creating special investigative groups, bringing together scholars of similar interests and opinions, and issuing reports. The funding of research has an especially important effect on what kinds of knowledge are developed. All of these methods are designed to promote the interests of the foundation.

The analysis of foundations begins with a determination of their general goals. Traditionally, foundations have supported social programs that maintain social stability. Foundations such as the Carnegie Corporation, the Ford Foundation, and the Rockefeller Foundation have promoted *welfare capitalism*. The basic tenet of welfare capitalism is that, to avoid serious social discontent in a capitalist society, it is necessary to intervene by giving aid to those in dire economic and social need. The general attitude of the large U.S. foundations is best expressed by Alan Pifer in his last report, issued in 1982, after serving eighteen years as president of the Carnegie Corporation. Pifer warns that without welfare capitalism,

> there lies nothing but increasing hardship for ever-growing numbers, a mounting possibility of severe social unrest, and the consequent development among the upper classes and the business community of sufficient fear for the survival of our capitalist economic system to bring about an abrupt change of course. Just as we built the general welfare state in the 1930s and expanded it in the 1960s as a safety valve for the easing of social tension, so will we do it again in the 1980s. Any other path is simply too risky.[17]

For the welfare state, education is an important means of maintaining social stability and filling the needs of capitalism. One source of social stability is the promise that education will provide equal opportunity for all people. Also, as indicated in Pifer's statement, the welfare state was expanded in the 1960s in order to control the wave of unrest among poor people in the United States. A key element of that expansion was the introduction of educational programs designed to break the cycle of poverty.[18]

In the early 1980s, the Carnegie Corporation was concerned about the faltering American educational system which, according to the critics, was causing the U.S. economy to fall behind those of West Germany and Japan. Thus, the primary issue was to shore up a failing capitalist economy by producing a better-educated labor force in the schools.

The opening statement of the Carnegie report on teaching reflects the basic needs of welfare capitalism. First, it recognizes that poor and minority groups will continue to have economic problems in a rapidly changing technological world. The report states, "As the world economy changes shape, it would be fatal to assume that America can succeed if only a portion of our school children succeed." The report emphasizes that by the year 2000 one out of every three Americans will be a member of a minority group and that currently one out of every four children is born in a state of poverty. Stressing the consequences of this situation, the report warns, "it is increasingly difficult for the poorly educated to find jobs. A growing number of permanently unemployed people seriously strains our social fabric." [19]

In addition, the report voices concern about the supply of well-trained workers: "A heavily technology-based economy will be unable to invest vast sums to maintain people who cannot contribute to the nation's productivity. American business already spends billions of dollars a year retraining people who arrive at the workplace with inadequate education."

Therefore, from the standpoint of welfare capitalism, improving the quality of teachers—which is the intention of the report—will result in better-trained workers. Better-trained workers, in turn, will be able to find jobs, thus reducing the social tensions caused by unemployment and saving the corporations millions of dollars in training-program costs.

In many cases, as in this report, foundations and corporations share the same interests. Better-educated workers and reduced job-training costs are primary issues for corporations. Also, the business sector wants people with well-trained, analytical minds. This desire is reflected in the task force statement, "The skills needed now are not routine. Our economy will be increasingly dependent on people who have a good intuitive grasp of the ways in which all kinds of physical and social systems work." [20]

The third interest group in education, the teachers' unions, is represented on the task force by their presidents, Albert Shanker of the American Federation of Teachers (AFT) and Mary Futrell of the National Education Association (NEA). Both unions support raising teacher salaries, raising the status of the profession, and increasing teacher autonomy. On the other hand, they are divided over merit pay and career ladders. Consequently, the two presidents have different opinions about the report. Albert Shanker gives complete approval to the contents of the report. Mary Futrell objects to the proposal for career ladders. She writes that the task force's recommendation for lead teachers, "suggests that some teachers are more equal than others. And it is not adequately differentiated from the flawed and failed merit-pay and job-ladder plans." [21]

Futrell's statement refers to specific proposals in the report. Briefly, the task force proposes the establishment of a national board of certification for teachers that would lay down standards for teacher training and certification. Most board members would be elected by holders of board certificates. The board is to issue two types of certificates: one for regular teachers and one for advanced teachers. These two certificates would be tied to a hierarchy of teaching positions: lead teachers, advanced certificate holders, certified teachers, and licensed teachers not yet certified by the board.

A unique feature of the Carnegie proposal is to increase teacher autonomy and professionalism by changing the organization of the school. The position of school principal would be eliminated and lead teachers would manage the schools and hire business administrators. This would replace the traditional hierarchical model of school governance, in which orders flow from the top to the teachers at the bottom, with a collegial model of decision making. In addition, the proposed model for teacher education would have the teacher act as an autonomous decision maker.

These changes would also be matched by a new salary scale that would range from a top of $72,000 for lead teachers to a bottom of $18,000 for teachers prior to certification by the national board. In addition, teachers would be rewarded by a form of merit pay based on improved student performance.

Both teachers' unions are interested in proposals to increase teacher autonomy and professionalism. Over the years, the unions have considered school administrators to be their major antagonists. The proposal to abolish the position of principal and establish schools operated by lead teachers would change employer-employee relationships in a direction favorable to teacher professionalism.

On the other hand, the unions are divided over the issues of a differentiated profession and merit pay. Historically, teachers have been paid according to a democratic scale, with increases in salary based on seniority and education. Attempts to introduce merit pay have resulted in charges that school administrators would show favoritism and that the ranks of teachers would be divided. An important feature of a democratic pay scale is the creation of unity and solidarity over pay issues. All salaries rise and fall equally, depending on the outcome of collective bargaining.

While the NEA, under the leadership of Mary Futrell, has fought career ladders and merit pay, the AFT, under the leadership of Albert Shanker, accepts these changes as necessary to win corporate support for schools. It is Shanker's belief that the future of public schooling depends on an alliance with the business community. Shanker's political strategy includes the acceptance of merit pay and career ladders in order to win support for higher salaries. Ironically, this means forging a link between organized labor and business in order to create a united interest group.

Shanker argues that one of the major accomplishments of the 1980s reforms was "the new and productive involvement of the business community in support of public education." He warns that the rejection of merit pay or career ladders by teachers would threaten this new support. "Outright rejection," Shanker writes, "of merit pay or of any other reform proposal could very well lead our newfound allies in the business community to the conclusion that public schools cannot be changed, that the bureaucracy is too rigid, teacher unions too powerful." Shanker fears that offending "the business community might lead not only to a loss of its vital support, but to its outright opposition; to abandonment of public schools in favor of other alternatives such as private schools, through tax credits or vouchers." [22]

The split between the two teachers' unions is the weakest element in the work of the task force. Essentially, the Carnegie Corporation hoped to build a strong coalition of the three major interest groups in education. This was achieved to a limited extent between the foundations, corporations, and the AFT. But Mary Futrell questioned merit pay and differentiated teaching positions, the proposed model of teacher education, and the national certification board.

The Carnegie Task Force report provides an example of conflict and cooperation among interest groups. Also, it is a model of how interest-group strategies can affect the political structure. For example, the report was issued with full media coverage. Later on, local school districts will have to be persuaded to hire teachers certified by the proposed national board. The report recommends that "state authorities should begin drafting plans to offer districts incentives to engage such teachers in appropriate roles and at higher rates of pay than teachers without board certification." [23] In addition, the board recommends that states take steps to ensure the equitable distribution of board-certified teachers.

In addition to the "big three," interest groups include other educational organizations, taxpayer groups, and single-issue organizations. The concerns of single-issue groups can range from school prayer to the inclusion of courses on state history in the curriculum. Also, foundations can emphasize a variety of viewpoints. Large foundations generally are concerned with maintaining welfare capitalism. Many smaller foundations, however, follow the social philosophies of their founders. Some, like the Heritage Foundation, have played an important role in shaping government policies. The Heritage Foundation, unlike the Carnegie Corporation, favors decreasing the role of government in education and ending social welfare programs. The foundation helped the Reagan administration staff the Department of Education after the 1980 election.[24]

The example of the Carnegie Corporation and the activities of other interest groups highlight the political nature of American education. Many groups compete to shape the educational system in a direction that serves their interests. At times groups work together, and at other times they are in conflict. Politicans, both elected and educational, are under continuous pressure from a variety of interest groups. Sometimes they seek the aid and support of these groups. Whatever the situation, interest groups play a major role in determining the organization and content of the American educational system.

THE KNOWLEDGE INDUSTRY

The knowledge industry supplies ideologies that not only justify the actions of politicians and interest groups but determine the methods and content of instruction in the schools. Of course, the creation and distribution of knowledge is the primary purpose of the educational system. But, like other parts of the system, political decisions determine the types of knowledge to be created and distributed.

The knowledge industry is comprised of funding agencies, researchers, knowledge brokers, testing organizations, and the publishing industry. Table 1.2 divides these components of the knowledge industry into three categories.

As mentioned above, political decisions are a major factor in the creation and distribution of knowledge in the United States. These political decisions are complex because of the variety of political

TABLE 1.2 THE KNOWLEDGE INDUSTRY

Creators
  Funding agencies
  Researchers
Gatekeepers
  Knowledge brokers
  Testing organizations
Distributors
  Textbook publishing
  Scholarly publishing

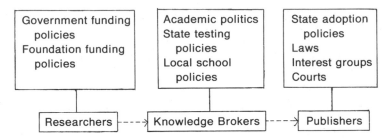

FIGURE 1.1 MAJOR POLITICAL INFLUENCES ON THE PRODUCTION AND DISTRIBUTION OF KNOWLEDGE

influences in each of the categories listed in Table 1.2. For instance, as illustrated in Figure 1.1, researchers depend on support from policy-directed funding agencies. The two major sources of funding are the federal government and private foundations. Each supports research that fulfills the policy goals of the specific organization. Also, gatekeepers are influenced by political decisions. (*Gatekeepers* are individuals and organizations that influence the distribution of research and new knowledge.) Many knowledge brokers are to be found in academia and government, worlds that have their own priorities and power struggles. (A *knowledge broker* is a research scholar who has a major influence on the decisions of national organizations and government agencies.)

The other major gatekeeper, testing organizations, has increasingly fallen under the influence of state and national political groups. Many states and local school districts rely on standardized tests for a variety of purposes, including teacher certification, high school graduation, and promotion between grade levels. Often, the content of tests determines the content of instruction. And finally, the publishing industry must deal with academic politics, state adoption policies, state laws, and court decisions. Since the early 1980s, many educational politicians have tried to use state adoption policies to determine the content of textbooks.

Federal Support of Educational Research

Federal support of educational research is an important element in the tangled web of political influence over the production and distribution of knowledge. Both government and foundation funding agencies must have some criteria for determining the types of research to be supported. Sometimes the criteria are based purely on the quality of the research proposal. However, in most cases, a prior determination has been made about the type of research to be funded.

Since the 1960s, the federal government has expanded its involvement in educational research. For instance, in 1960 the combined state and local educational research expenditures were $7.76 million, foundation expenditures were $6 million, and federal expenditures were $19.2 million, or 58 percent of the total. In 1965, the federal government increased its support of educational research to $69.8 million, while state and local expenditures increased to $14 million, and foundation expenditures increased to $14.4 million. By 1965 the federal government was providing more than 71 percent of the money for educational research in the United States.[25]

Of course, the research community has hoped that federal support would be given with no strings attached. But that was impossible because of the political issues surrounding educational policies. Federal research priorities have shifted with changes in administration. In the 1960s, research support emphasized educating the poor and disadvantaged. The 1970s saw a shift to career and vocational education and competency and mastery learning.

The most important step in the politicization of research policy was taken in the 1980 national elections, when both Democrats and Republicans had clearly defined educational constituencies. Each constituency promoted its own educational agenda, which would have consequences for research policies. With the election of a Republican administration in 1980, funds for educational research were cut back, and the research agenda included tuition tax credits and vouchers.

Foundation-Sponsored Research

Just as the political agenda of any given administration determines what research will be pursued, the policy agenda of a foundation determines what research it will support. In the Carnegie Task Force report, research money was directed toward developing an evaluation method for selecting and certifying lead teachers. Obviously, any evaluation model instituted by a national certification board would have a profound effect on teacher training. Colleges would need to educate teachers to do well in the evaluation process.

The Carnegie report provides an example of the chain of activities that affects the development of new knowledge. In this case, concern with the possible social tensions arising from unemployment and poverty, the poor performance of the United States in international markets, and the complaints of employers about the quality of high school graduates resulted in a focus on improving the quality of the teaching profession. In turn, this has created a need for an evaluation model that can be used by a national certification board. Consequently, the funding of research to develop an evaluation model will have a direct effect on the education of all teachers in the United States.

Knowledge Brokers

Government- and foundation-sponsored research is conducted primarily in universities, research-and-development institutes, and private research groups. Within these settings, knowledge brokers influence decisions about who receives research support, the types of research that are considered acceptable by the research community, and the types of research that are published in leading scholarly journals. For example, Richard Dershimer, former executive officer of the American Educational Research Association (AERA) writes, "Every research-and-development support program launched by the federal government was initiated by a small handful of persons—in other words, by a professional-bureaucratic elite."[26] The launching of these support programs occurred in the context of the broad political goals of the federal administration.

Knowledge brokers are part of the professional-bureaucratic elite discussed by Dershimer. Within the educational research community, the most important interest group is the American Educational Research Association (AERA). The leaders of this organization play important roles as knowledge brokers. In addition, direct linkages have existed between the organization and the federal bureaucracies. During the 1980s, these linkages were disrupted when the Reagan administration reduced the funding for research and tried to establish a different research agenda.

In addition to the leadership of AERA, other knowledge brokers can be found at universities that receive the most research money. In the mid-1980s, under the leadership of Judith Lanier, dean of the college of education at Michigan State University, the Holmes Group was formed for the purposes of reforming and dominating teacher education. One self-proclaimed objective of the group is to organize the major research universities into a national lobbying group.[27]

The Testing Industry

The second important gatekeeper is the testing industry. During the 1970s and 1980s, standardized testing became increasingly important in measuring school effectiveness and in determining the certification of teachers. During the 1970s, the accountability movement relied on standardized tests such as the California and Stanford achievement tests. The accountability movement arose as a result of demands by many community groups for more public control of the schools. School administrators responded by distributing the results of standardized tests in their communities. Later in the 1970s, the More Effective Schools movement measured effectiveness according to gains on standardized tests. An important goal of the More Effective Schools movement was to make the school principal responsible for the quality of instruction and at least partly responsible for students' gains and losses on standardized tests. Consequently, in many communities principals are rated by the performance of their students on standardized achievement tests. In addition, some experiments during the 1980s with merit pay for teachers relied on standardized student test scores.[28]

A logical consequence of relying on standardized achievement tests is that the content of the tests determines the content of instruction. Currently, no statistics are available on the number of school principals who have told their staffs to emphasize certain topics because those topics appear in standardized tests. Principals and teachers are obviously acting in their own self-interest when they gear their teaching to such tests.

The same argument applies to the increased reliance on standardized testing for teacher certification. When the teaching profession was reformed in the 1980s, some states developed their own teacher tests for certification or relied on the National Teacher Examination published by the Educational Testing Service.

These tests function as gatekeepers of knowledge. Essentially, the test writers determine what knowledge is of greatest worth in any field of study. Most fields of study, however, are divided into various schools of thought, and there are frequent controversies about what knowledge is of the most value. Standardized tests may ignore such differences and arbitrarily decide what knowledge should be taught. In some situations, such "official knowledge" is determined not by scholars but by interest groups.

While testing organizations and knowledge brokers act as gatekeepers, the publishing industry acts as a distributor of knowledge. Publishers are primarily interested in making money in a highly competitive market. Publishers of elementary and secondary school textbooks must deal with a market that is influenced by censorship groups and state textbook commissions. College textbook and scholarly publishers, while still interested in making a profit, deal with knowledge brokers in the academic world.

The same political forces that influence the creation and distribution of knowledge also influence other parts of the educational system. Elected politicians, educational politicians, and school boards determine to a large degree the development of new knowledge and its dissemination. At all levels, interest groups shape the methods and content of schooling. What emerges from this process is research that justifies the policy positions of government and foundations, and bland textbooks that promulgate official knowledge.

CONCLUSION

Motivated by self-interest, educational ideals, and beliefs about correct educational practices, the major parts of the political system of American education interact at the local, state, and national levels. The complex web of tensions, conflicts, and ambitions among elected politicians, educational politicians, interest groups, and the knowledge industry keeps the educational system in a constant state of change and turmoil. One could argue that the major disease of the American education system is its constant propensity to change to serve the needs of various politicians and to solve economic and social problems.

A major cause of tension and conflict in the politics of schooling is the belief that education can serve political ends. People fight to control what is taught in the schools because they believe education can serve political and economic interests. The next chapter will analyze the political uses of schooling and will explain why the groups discussed in this chapter struggle for power over the educational system.

NOTES

1. Some moderate Republicans rejected the basic policies of the Reagan administration. For instance, Senator Lowell Weicker of Connecticut, a Republican and a member of the Labor, Education, and Health appropriations subcommittees, was critical of the Reagan administration's reductions in education spending. David Stockman, head of the Office of Management and Budget, called Weicker "one of the biggest spenders to bother calling himself a Republican this century"; *The Triumph of Politics: Why the Reagan Revolution Failed* (New York: Harper & Row, 1986), p. 372. A good description of the tensions within the Republican educational coalition can be found in Terrel Bell's "Educational Policy Development in the Reagan Administration," *Phi Delta Kappan*, Vol. 67, No. 7 (March 1986), 487–93.
2. Harry Summerfield, *Power and Process: the Formulation and Limits of Federal Educational Policy* (Berkeley, Calif.: McCutcheon, 1974).
3. See Susan Fuhrman's "State-level Politics and School Financing," in Nelda Cambron-McCabe and Allan Oden, eds., *The Changing Politics of School Finance* (Cambridge, Mass.: Ballinger, 1982).
4. Bell, "Education Policy Development."
5. Ibid., p. 488.
6. Stockman, *Triumph of Politics*, p. 372.

7. Bill Honig, *Last Chance for Our Children: How You Can Help Save Our Schools* (Reading, Mass.: Addison-Wesley, 1985), pp. 109–26.
8. For a discussion of career- and place-oriented superintendents, see Ernest R. House, *The Politics of Educational Innovation* (Berkeley: McCutchan, 1974), pp. 37–44.
9. The social composition of American school boards is published in the January issues of the *American School Board Journal.*
10. For a study of the role of local elites in school politics, see Kathryn Borman and Joel Spring, *Schools in Central Cities* (White Plains, N.Y.: Longman, 1984), pp. 46–75.
11. For a study of the court struggle for desegregation, see Richard Kluger, *Simple Justice* (New York: Random House, 1975).
12. For a discussion of these court cases, see Joel Spring, *American Education*, 3rd ed. (White Plains, N.Y.: Longman, 1985), pp. 235–65.
13. For instance, desegregation was aided by the 1964 Civil Rights Act, equal rights for the handicapped was aided by Public Law 94–142, and children for whom English was a second language were aided by the Bilingual Education Act of 1968.
14. For the classic description of this symbiotic relationship, see Theodore J. Lowi, *The End of Liberalism: The Second Republic of the United States* (New York: Norton, 1979), pp. 22–42.
15. Stockman, *Triumph of Politics*, p. 120.
16. Task Force on Teaching as a Profession, *A Nation Prepared: Teachers for the 21st Century* (New York: Carnegie Corporation of New York, 1986).
17. Alan Pifer, "When Fashionable Rhetoric Fails," *Education Week*, 23 February 1983, p. 24.
18. See Waldemar Nielsen, *The Big Foundations* (New York: Columbia University Press, 1972).
19. Carnegie Task Force, *A Nation Prepared*, p. 14.
20. Ibid., p. 20.
21. Ibid., p. 117.
22. Albert Shanker, "Teachers and Reform," in Philip G. Altbach et al., eds., *Excellence in Education: Perspectives on Policy and Practice* (Buffalo, N.Y.: Prometheus Books, 1985), pp. 203–17.
23. Carnegie Task Force, *A Nation Prepared*, p. 13.
24. For critical studies of different foundations, see Robert Arnove, ed., *Philanthropy and Cultural Imperialism: The Foundations at Home and Abroad* (Bloomington: Indiana University Press, 1982).
25. Lee J. Cronbach and Patrick Suppes, eds., *Research for Tomorrow's Schools* (London: Collier-Macmillan, 1969), p. 205.
26. Richard A. Dershimer, *The Federal Government and Education R & D* (Lexington, Mass.: Lexington Press, 1976), p. 2.
27. Holmes Group, *Tomorrow's Teachers: A Report of the Holmes Group* (East Lansing, Mich.: Holmes Group, 1986).
28. The classic book on the More Effective Schools movement is Michael Rutter et al., *Fifteen Thousand Hours* (Cambridge, Mass.: Harvard University Press, 1979).

CHAPTER 2

Causes of Conflict

The causes of conflict in education are as complex as its political structure. Each part of the political organization of schooling has its own set of interests and ideologies. Sometimes these interests and ideologies are shared, and sometimes they are held by one particular part of the political structure. Conflict occurs as different groups attempt to have the educational system serve their own interests and ideologies.

For the purposes of analysis, a distinction will be made between external and internal conflict. *External conflict* refers to struggles between individuals and groups outside the administrative structure of education. External conflict can originate with politicians, special-interest groups, and groups identified with a particular ethnic culture, religion, political belief, or social class. As indicated in Table 2.1, the major issues involved in external conflict over education are culture, language, religion, curriculum content, curriculum organization, educational opportunities, and educational funding.

Internal conflict occurs primarily over power and money and involves teachers, administrators, and the knowledge industry.

The actors involved in external and internal conflict sometimes share the same interests. For instance, an external group might want to increase its political power by promoting its ethnic identity through bilingual education. Within the educational structure, it will find allies among bilingual educators who want to promote bilingual education in order to protect their jobs, increase their incomes, and retain what they believe to be the best method of language instruction. In this situation, different sets of interests would unite external and internal groups against critics of bilingual education.

The following sections describe conflicts that occur when external

TABLE 2.1 CAUSES OF POLITICAL CONFLICT IN EDUCATION

Causes of External Conflict	
Culture	Curriculum
Language	Increasing educational opportunities
Religion	Funding of education

Causes of Internal Conflict	
Power	
Money	

groups struggle to control education in order to maintain or gain political and economic power, and when internal groups struggle for increased power and income.

EXTERNAL CAUSES OF CONFLICT

Politicians, individuals, and organized groups use schooling to gain political power and economic advantages. Education becomes a source of conflict when those in power use schooling to maintain their power or when those out of power use it to gain power. In the United States, such struggles have centered on minority cultures, religion, and the content of the curriculum.

The following hypothetical situation depicts the possible relationships between education and political power. Consider a totalitarian nation composed of several cultural, linguistic, and religious groups, and ruled by an elite that shares a common culture, language, and religion. The ruling elite tries to perpetuate its political power by having only its culture, religion, and language taught in government-operated schools. Schoolchildren are left with the impression that the elite culture, language, and religion are superior to all others in the nation.

In addition, children of the elite are more successful in school because their home culture and language are the same as the school's. To further create a sense of superiority among elite children, the schools claim to give everyone equal access to either a vocational or a college preparatory curriculum. Because their language and culture differ from that of the schools, nonelite groups perform poorly and, as a result, are tracked into the vocational curriculum. Children of nonelite groups believe they are intellectually inferior to elite children because they are in vocational studies and, consequently, condemned to spend their lives in the lower levels of the economic system.

In this totalitarian state, the political content of the curriculum includes patriotic exercises and a national history and literature that emphasizes the role of the elite. In addition, the curriculum touts the superiority of the country's economic and political system and proclaims the inferiority of other political and economic systems.

This state of affairs might be difficult to maintain because knowledge carries with it the seeds of rebellion. In fact, one could argue that the best way to maintain political control is to deny schooling to all children except those of the elite. In the modern world, this would be difficult because industry requires educated workers. A modern totalitarian state can not maintain its economic system if it excludes large sections of the population from the educational system. Consequently, a major conflict in modern educational systems arises between elites, who want to use schooling to control the population, and the dispossessed, who want to use it to advance their social, political, and economic rights.

This tension results from the fact that, in varying degrees, education increases an individual's knowledge and ability to think. Thus any attempt to maintain political control through schooling carries with it the potential for rebellion. Increased knowledge and mental ability to breed resistance to control. As Henry Giroux argues, pockets of resistance will severely hinder attempts to dominate[1]

The educational practices of our hypothetical totalitarian state contain many forms of control that, when exercised in real situations, have sparked conflict around the world. For instance, educational conflict often occurs when several ethnic or religious groups exist within a political system. Elite groups will impose their culture and religion in the schools in order to establish their cultural superiority and, more important, to destroy the cohesiveness of other cultural groups. Cultural groups that lack cohesiveness are not able to form organizations in opposition to the ruling elite. This is what happened in the colonial era, when colonial powers exerted cultural domination through language and educational policies. For instance, European nations made their languages the official language of their colonies. In addition, attendance in their educational systems provided the only route to government positions. Such policies had several effects. First, the colonized were taught that their culture was inferior to that of European nations; they were expected to be grateful for the right to participate and to learn from a superior culture. Second, access to political power depended on absorbing the culture of the European power.[2]

Language

In countries with diverse language groups, language policies are a common means of maintaining political power. China is a good example of how a nation's language policies can vary with changes in its political goals. Following the communist revolution in the 1940s, the government faced the problem of creating national unity among differing language and cultural groups living on the border between China and the Soviet Union. At first, the government, hoping to achieve interethnic solidarity, improved educational opportunities and translation capabilities for ethnic groups. Improved translation capabilities—that is, the translation of the majority's literature and political documents into local ethnic languages—were intended to increase the influence of the majority culture.[3]

A policy reversal occurred in the 1960s when heightened tension between China and the Soviet Union caused border groups to demand separate-nation status. To assure that these ethnic groups remained in China, the central government reduced the power of minority elites by limiting the use of minority languages and emphasizing the role of class struggle. The use of the majority language in the schools, as opposed to the minority language, was designed to reduce ethnic identity. Education in class struggle was intended to cause minority members to resist their ethnic leaders. Overall, the major goal of the Chinese government was to promote assimilation by teaching the majority language and culture in all schools. These antiminority policies continued throughout the Cultural Revolution that occurred during the mid-1960s and mid-1970s; through such policies, revolutionary literature was made available to minority groups.

In the mid-1970s, the Chinese government's concentration on industrial modernization resulted in yet another change in language and cultural policies. To meet the demands of industrial modernization, educational policy emphasized education for economic growth. Suddenly, science and mathematics became more important than revolutionary and political literature. Since cooperation from ethnic groups was required for economic development to occur, the Chinese government adopted a friendly attitude toward local languages and cultures. As a result, ethnic pride was emphasized and constitutional protection was given to minority languages. In addition, institutes were established for the study of ethnic languages and literature.

The example of China demonstrates how language and cultural policies can change to need general policy goals. The events of June 16, 1976, in the township of Soweto, South Africa, provide an example of how language policies in the schools can lead to political violence. The

South African government, as part of its general policy of dominating blacks, decreed the use of the white Afrikaans language in black schools. Following the decree, thousands of black students protested in the streets. In response, South African police shot a 13-year-old black boy, causing an uprising and the radicalization of an entire generation of black students.[4]

Language policies have also become a source of conflict in the United States. For instance, during the Reagan administration, bilingual education created much controversy. During this period a conflict occurred between the Chicano community, which believed that bilingual education strengthened its cultural identity, and groups wanting to make English the official language of the United States. Chicano leaders believed that a strong ethnic identity would increase their political support.

The two major U.S. political parties are divided over bilingual education. Traditionally, organized ethnic groups, including Chicanos, have been a strong force in the Democratic party. In contrast, Republicans have felt threatened by many organized ethnic groups. Consequently, bilingual education became a major target of attack during the Reagan administration. In fact, some members of the Republican party joined a movement opposing bilingual education and supporting the adoption of English as the official language of the United States. Making English the official language would weaken organized ethnic politics and ensure the continued domination of the majority culture. The movement for making English the official language was led by an organization, U.S. English, founded in 1983 by S. I. Hayakawa, a former Republican Senator.

In 1986, in reaction to the Reagan administration, the National Association of Bilingual Education increased its political activities and intensified its public relations efforts. In reference to S. I. Hayakawa and U.S. English, Gene T. Chavez, the president of the association, warned that "those who think this country can only tolerate one language" were motivated more by political than by educational concerns. At the same meeting, the incoming president of the organization, Chicago school administrator José Gonzalez, attacked the Reagan administration and the Department of Education for entering an "unholy alliance" with right-wing groups opposing bilingual education, groups such as U.S. English, Save Our Schools, and the Heritage Foundation.[5]

Within the Reagan administration, Secretary of Education William Bennett attempted to reduce support for bilingual education by appointing opponents of it to the government's National Advisory and Coordinating Council on Bilingual Education. The new appointees expressed a preference for immersing non-English-speaking children in the English language, rather than teaching them in a bilingual context. In addition, the new appointees favored giving more power to local officials to determine programs. Of course, such a policy would undercut the power that the Chicano community had gained by working with the federal government. Originally, Chicanos had turned to the federal government for assistance because they lacked power in local politics.[6]

Religion

Religious groups often use education for purposes of cultural domination. Even in countries with a single religion, differing sects will attempt to impose their point of view in the schools. For instance, a historic struggle continues in Israel between Orthodox and liberal Jews. At the heart of this struggle is the effort to gain political control of the Israeli government. Orthodox Jews, in contrast to liberal Jews, wish to impose stricter standards of morality. In 1986 Orthodox Jews burned bus stops to protest a revealing bathing-suit advertisement. In response, liberal Jews attacked Orthodox houses of worship. Some Jews complained that the intolerance of Orthodox Jews was causing many liberal Jews to emigrate to the United States.

In response to charges that they were responsible for driving young Jews out of the country, Orthodox Jews claimed that the real problem was the lack of moral teaching in the elementary and high school curriculum. In a letter to the *New York Times Magazine*, R. Ben-Chaim of the Orthodox KACH movement in Israel blamed secular Jews for creating a school curriculum devoid of traditional Jewish values. He linked the migration of young Jews to the United States to the teaching of materialistic values in the schools. The answer to this religious and political struggle, he wrote, "is to infuse the Israeli educational system with a hearty dose of traditional Judaism."[7]

Religion is also a major source of political conflict in the United States. Problems regarding culture and religion date back to the beginnings of the common school movement in the nineteenth century. As Carl Kaestle argues, a primary reason for establishing the common-school system was to insure that the Protestant republican culture would prevail over the Catholic immigrant culture. Resisting this attempt at religious and cultural domination, Catholics organized a system of schools that more closely reflected the cultural values of new immigrant groups.[8] Throughout the nineteenth century and into the twentieth, both Catholics and Protestants often referred to the U.S. public schools as "Protestant schools."

By the middle of the twentieth century, political elites were no longer primarily Protestant but contained a mixture of religious groups. Consequently, there was a growing movement to remove all religious content from the schools and achieve religious neutrality, which resulted in the school prayer and Bible decisions by the U.S. Supreme Court in the 1960s. These decisions declared it unconstitutional to read the Bible in schools for religious purposes and to conduct school prayers.[9]

Some religious groups were infuriated by the Supreme Court decisions. Historically correct, these religious groups argued that American public schools had always emphasized Christian morality. But the Court's decisions symbolized that the ruling culture of America was no longer dominated by Protestant ideology. Not only did the election of President John F. Kennedy in 1960 demonstrate that Catholics had joined the ranks of the political elite, but that public statements on morality were losing their religious tone and becoming increasingly secular.

The result was a sharp political reaction from Protestant fundamentalist groups, who saw themselves displaced from the dominant American culture. These groups attacked the public schools in the 1970s for teaching *secular humanism*. According to them, secular humanism taught individuals to rely on their own ability to interpret human events and make decisions, as opposed to relying on the authority of God.

While some Protestant groups abandoned the public schools in the 1970s, others joined a political campaign to restore traditional Christian values in the schools. The Protestants who abandoned the public schools established private Christian schools, which in the 1970s became the fastest-growing private-school system in America.[10]

The political goals of the campaign to restore traditional Christian values in the public schools included increasing parental control of schooling, amending the Constitution to allow school prayer, and expelling all signs of secular humanism from the public-school curriculum. Eventually, these groups supported the Republican party because President Reagan had promised to restore school prayer and support tuition tax credit legislation that would have provided funding for private Christian schools.

In addition to membership in a dominant religious and language group, one's admission to elite status depends on one's access to particular cultural knowledge. For instance, in England and the United States in the nineteenth century, knowledge of classical languages and literature, while having little practical value, created a distinct cultural difference between the upper and lower classes.

Knowledge of classical literature and languages was gained through attending elite schools. Public opinion tended to accept the idea that a person with a classical education was superior to other members of society.

Of course, in the twentieth century in the United States, language usage and cultural knowledge are important for success in school and for gaining access to the upper class. Minority groups have had to choose between maintaining their ethnic identity in order to have an organized political base, and assimilating to the majority culture in order to advance socially. The tension between these two positions is a major issue in debates about minority education and politics in the twentieth century.[11]

The Political Content of the School Curriculum

In a totalitarian society it is possible to teach a single interpretation of the laws and government in the public schools. But in a society such as that of the United States, which fosters a variety of political beliefs and interpretations of the functions of government, attempts to teach principles of government can result in major political battles.

Ironically, conflict over the political content of instruction has produced a curriculum noted for its blandness and lack of controversy. An inherent problem for public schools in a democratic society is the necessity of accommodating a wide variety of viewpoints. With regard to political issues, public schools open the door for attack from opposition groups when they present any one political viewpoint. Consequently, school administrators tend to take the safe route by not presenting anything that might provoke attacks by outside groups.

Horace Mann, often called the father of the American common school, feared that the teaching of any political content in the classroom might destroy the public schools; political factions would compete, each demanding that their interpretation dominate classroom teaching. On the other hand, Mann believed that political stability depended on the teaching of republican principles of government. His solution was to teach only noncontroversial aspects of the functioning of government and to avoid issues open to dispute.[12] Ironically, in a society that prizes open political debate, fear of controversy over political teachings in the classroom, along with market forces that influence the publication of textbooks, have created bland, uncontroversial social studies classes.

Related to the political content of the curriculum is the use of schools to build emotional attachments to the groups that hold political power. Most governments of the world, in varying degrees, use national educational systems for this purpose. Normally, the goal is to create a love of country or government. This is accomplished by having schoolchildren sing patriotic songs, recite a loyalty pledge or pledge of allegiance, study a highly patriotic form of the nation's history, participate in nationalistic ceremonies, and study the national literature. For some governments, the ideal is to instill in citizens such a strong love of their country that they are willing to die in war for its preservation.

The Differentiated Curriculum

Conflict is caused by using a differentiated curriculum to divide students into college-bound and vocational tracks. Obviously, corporations have wanted the schools to produce a properly trained work force. In addition, the separation of students into different curriculum tracks reinforces and perpetuates social-class and cultural differences.

Throughout the twentieth century, in the United States and other countries, lower-class students have been channeled into vocational and technical curricula, while upper-class students have been channeled into college preparatory curricula. Assuming that a relationship exists between social class and political power, such differentiation does not provide lower-class students with the knowledge required to exercise political power. For upper-class students, differentiation guarantees their continued position in the political elite.

In the United States, the differentiated curriculum has been a target of attack since the famous debates between Booker T. Washington and W. E. B. DuBois. Washington argued that an industrial education would integrate blacks into the nation's economic system. DuBois, on the other hand, argued that an industrial education would perpetuate black economic enslavement. Washington's argument resulted both in different curricula for black and white students, and in segregated schools.[13]

The debate over differentiated curricula continued through the twentieth century. In the 1980s the idea was attacked by Mortimer Adler, who argued that separate curricula were undemocratic because they deny equal access to knowledge to all students. He argued that students channeled into vocational studies receive an education that has less political and economic value than that received by those preparing for college. According to Adler, a truly democratic education gives everyone the same fund of knowledge and intellectual skills.[14]

Increasing Educational Opportunities

Education can be used by those in power as a means of political control and it can be used by those not in power to gain access to political control. Sometimes, the tension between the two gives rise to a political struggle to control the educational system. For instance, segregated schools in the Southern states ensured the continued political and economic domination of whites over blacks. On the other side of the issue, the black struggle for integrated education was part of a broader movement to enhance their political power and economic advantages. At the center of white and black concerns was the issue of gaining control over the educational system.

Traditionally, four major positions are taken regarding the expansion of educational opportunities to the general population. The most conservative position opposes the expansion of education opportunities because it might undermine the obedience of the lower class to the upper class and make the lower class unwilling to work at menial occupations. Another position, which also protects the interests of the upper class, is to seek expanded opportunities for the lower class so that they can be educated for obedience and for their place in society. The third position is to justify expanded educational opportunities because they supply citizens with the knowledge to protect their political and economic interests. Finally, one can argue that if the government provides schools, then justice requires that schools should be provided equally to all citizens.

For instance, in the early nineteenth century Workingmen's parties in New York, Massachusetts, and Pennsylvania campaigned for free common schools. Their emphasis in the campaign differed from that of other leaders of the common-school movement, who wanted schools that would instill common political and moral values and reduce tensions between the rich and the poor. The Workingmen's parties wanted schools to arm workers with knowledge to protect their economic and political rights. While the activities of the Workingmen's parties contributed to the eventual creation of common schools, differences continued to exist between social classes over the goals of the schools.[15]

Similar tensions over the expansion and the goals of education occurred in the South after the Civil War. Many white Southern planters did not want educational opportunities provided for the freed black population out of a fear that educated blacks would be dissatisfied with menial work and therefore difficult to control. On the other hand, whites interested in industrial expansion in the South in the late nineteenth century believed expanded educational opportunities were necessary to build an industrial work force.[16]

Also, divisions existed between blacks themselves. Under the leadership of Booker T. Washington, many blacks agreed that expanded educational opportunities for blacks would occur only if they accepted segregated schools and industrial education. In opposition to Booker T. Washington, W. E. B. DuBois rejected this proposal and argued that education should prepare blacks to protect their political, social, and economic rights.[17]

While Washington's ideas triumphed in the nineteenth century, W. E. B. DuBois went on to help found the National Association for the Advancement of Colored People (NAACP), which struggled throughout the twentieth century to end segregated schooling. The conflict over segregated education was the most intense struggle for expanded educational opportunities in the United States in the twentieth century.

In recent years in the United States, the legal struggle over equal educational opportunity is a major factor in expanding educational opportunities for the handicapped, special learners, women, and racial and linguistic minorities. The heart of the legal issue is the Fourteenth Amendment to the Constitution, which provides equal protection before the law. As interpreted by the Supreme Court, the Fourteenth Amendment guarantees that if a state provides a service such as education, then all citizens must have equal access to the service.

For years, handicapped people complained that they were denied equal access to education because school buildings had not been constructed to meet their physical needs and to accommodate wheelchairs. In addition, they argued that the particular problems faced by the physically handicapped and those with learning problems were not being considered in school programs. Also, those children for whom English was a second language required special prorams if they were to receive equal educational opportunities in U.S. schools. Using the same legal reasoning, it was argued that women were being excluded from educational programs and opportunities.

From the 1950s to the 1980s, the struggle to end segregation in the United States and to meet the needs of groups requiring special attention involved a major expansion of educational opportunities. In fact, it was one of the primary sources of political conflict during this period. All parts of the political structure of American schooling were forced to deal with the issues raised in these conflicts.

Funding of Education

At the heart of the conflict over school finance are two questions: who should pay and who should receive the money. In the early nineteenth century, the issue of who should pay struck at the very core of the concept of common schooling. For instance, one could argue that only parents with children who used the schools should be required to support common schooling. It was legitimately asked why unmarried adults, married couples without children, and families who sent their children to private schools should be required to provide financial support to public schooling.

The answer given by nineteenth-century common-school reformers is still used to counter arguments against requiring all people to support public schooling. Today, many communities having large numbers of retirees without school-age children and large numbers of families with children attending parochial schools have difficulty raising money for public schools through local taxes. In response to their resistance against taxation, public leaders argue that schools benefit the entire public and not just the children who attend. This line of reasoning was used by common-school reformer Horace Mann in the nineteenth century. He argued that individual wealth depends on the general wealth of the community and that education, by increasing the productivity of the worker, increases the community's wealth. Therefore, while a childless person or parents who send their child to a private school might not receive direct benefits from public money spent on education, they do receive indirect benefits from the increased wealth resulting from the improved educational level of the community. Because the existence of public schools thus increases everyone's wealth, Horace Mann argued, all people should therefore pay for public education.[18] Today, under the banner of general welfare, public-school officials justify general support of the schools. Without public schools, educators and public officials argue, there would be higher crime rates, unemployment, and expanded welfare rolls.

In the United States, the reliance on property taxes to fund schools has made it easy for citizens to resist increases in local school taxes. Communities with large numbers of retirees and children in parochial schools can reduce their funding of public education by voting for low property taxes. This often creates major political problems in small communities, as public-school supporters pit themselves against those opposed to such spending.

Reliance on property taxes also creates another set of issues. It is argued that since businesses and corporations benefit from public schooling, they have an obligation to provide support. But because some corporations choose to locate in areas with small residential populations, they pay low property taxes. This occurs because school district boundaries define the areas of taxation. Therefore, some school districts have high property tax rates while others have low rates. Corporations, like individuals, often want lower taxes and will either locate in communities with low property tax rates or work to reduce them. Some corporations, however, might consider a good public school system an important asset and work for increased taxes.

The reliance on property taxes and the existence of school districts create political conflict. For instance, the district method of organiza tion makes it possible for rich school districts to exist next to poor ones. For example, one school district might have a strong industrial base with wealthy families in residence who are willing to provide strong financial support to local public schools. Since the community is wealthy, such support can be provided with little effort through local taxes. On the other hand, in an adjacent school district there could be a declining industrial base with large numbers of families living on welfare. In this situation, a high property tax rate is required to provide minimum funds for education.

In the 1970s, major political battles erupted over attempts to end the disparity between rich and poor school districts. As in many of the political battles in the United States, dispossessed groups had to seek redress for their complaints in the courts. The first major school finance case originated in California when a parent complained that he could improve the education of his children in the public schools only by moving to a wealthier school district. Because he could not afford housing in the wealthier district, he argued that reliance on property taxes raised in local school districts created unequal educational opportunities. The California supreme court agreed with this argument and in 1971, in *Serrano v. Priest*, declared the method of school finance in California unconstitutional according to the state constitution. Later, the U.S. Supreme Court ruled in a similar case, *Rodriguez v. San Antonio Independent School District* (1973), that school finance was not an issue under the U.S. Constitution and therefore had to be dealt with at the state level.

Consequently, in the 1970s state legislatures became embroiled in school finance reform. One result of this involvement was to strengthen the role of state legislatures in education. In addition, the issue of who should pay for public schooling became a major problem at the state level of government and an issue between various interest groups. For instance, most corporations resist increased corporate taxes to support education and favor reliance on lotteries and sales taxes.

Corporate resistance to taxation for schools is described in Ira Shor's *Culture Wars: School and Society in the Conservative Restoration, 1969–1984.* Shore argues that business leaders in the early 1980s, while campaigning for state school reform, saw to it that increased taxes resulting from reforms would fall primarily on the shoulders of the poor and the lower middle class. Shor writes, "Once public acceptance of the crisis and of official solutions emerged, it was time to present the bill. Regressive taxes were identified as the source of funds to finance school excellence." He argues that strong resistance to increased taxes was overcome by claims that the failure of the public schools was a major cause of economic decline. Once that argument was made, tax-increase plans spread from state to state. However, most of these plans avoided increasing corporate taxes and relied instead on regressive funding, particularly sales taxes and lotteries, that primarily affected the poor and the lower middle class. In Shore's words, "This strategy generated new revenues from the bottom in hard times, while protecting key constituencies at the top military-industrial complex, high-tech corporate profits, the rich and their tax loopholes, tax abatements for corporate construction in local areas, the oil depletion allowance, etc." [19]

Therefore one could conclude from Shor's argument that as a result of school finance reforms in the 1970s, corporations dominated school funding issues at the state level. Of course, whether this is true or not for a particular state depends on the power of other interest groups to affect the decisions of legislators and governors. Obviously, business groups favor regressive taxes, while politicians avoid unpopular increases in state income taxes. The tendency, because it often represents the path of least resistance, is to rely increasingly on regressive taxation. This can place a disproportionate amount of the tax burden for supporting public schools on the poor and the lower middle class.

Ira Shor accuses business interests of having adopted a Machiavellian attitude in the early 1980s. Rather than pay increased taxes, business interests gave their support directly to schools through grants, partnerships, and direct aid. Shor writes, "Businesses in the third-phase plan were called upon to 'do their part,' by getting more involved in schools, adopting poor districts like orphans, donating over-age equipment, offering excess supplies and furniture, and by lending experts to short-staffed departments. All this generosity was tax-deductible." [20]

School finance reform also opened the door to battles over how state monies should be spent on education. As a result, teachers' unions were often pitted against corporate interests. Ideally, corporations want to improve schools at the lowest cost, while teachers' unions campaign for more money for education, particularly for teachers' salaries. One condition that aided teachers' unions was the increasing shortage of teachers. Historically, teachers' salaries have followed a supply-and-demand curve. In the past, a shortage of teachers coupled with high demand has resulted in real increases in teachers' incomes. During the 1970s, the reverse of these conditions brought about a decline in real wages. In the 1980s increasing demand and declining supply created hope in the teachers' unions for a real increase in wages.

Business groups responded to this situation by calling for selective salary increases. From the perspective of business, educational costs could be kept down only if selected teachers—not all teachers—received wage increases. Consequently, business leaders and politicians in the 1980s campaigned for merit pay and career ladders.[21] As Ira Shor writes, "Management wanted to reallocate selectively the teacher wage package so that math and science teachers were paid more, out of a seemingly neutral, merit-based system. The overall wage package would increase slightly, financed by regressive taxation on sales, income, and property of householders."[22]

In addition to corporate and teacher interest groups fighting over government money for education, private-school groups have demanded their share. In the 1970s and 1980s, private-school groups were politically active in supporting tuition tax credits and vouchers. Both *tuition tax credits*, which would allow parents to credit educational expenses against their income taxes, and *vouchers*, which would give them a grant of money to be spent on education, have been promoted as ways to increase educational choice. Several arguments have been advanced for these plans. One argument is that more choices will increase competition, which will raise the quality of public schools. Second, parents whose children attend private schools are unfairly burdened by having to pay both taxes to support public schools and tuition to private-schools. And last, vouchers or tuition tax credits would give the poor the right to choose a private education.

Of course, the public-school lobby views tuition tax credits and vouchers as a threat. Teachers' unions strongly oppose any legislation favoring financial incentives to promote choice at the state and national levels. On the other hand, Catholic and Protestant private schools have pressed hard in state capitals and in Congress for tuition tax credits and voucher legislation. On the national level, this conflict over government subsidies of choice in education has been partly responsible for the teachers' unions aligning with the Democrats and to private-school groups aligning with the Republicans.

In the future, school finance will continue to play a major role in educational politics. At the core of the political struggle will be the issues of who should pay and how the money should be spent. Teachers' unions, corporate interest groups, and private-school groups will continue to be the major actors involved in this conflict.

INTERNAL CAUSES OF CONFLICT

Power and money are at the heart of most conflicts within the educational establishment. Educational administrators struggle to protect or improve their positions within the eductional bureaucracy, teachers struggle against administrators to gain money and power, and the knowledge industries compete for profits. In the context of this intricate interweaving of conflicts, members of the educational establishment reach out to make alliances with politicians, interest groups, and the general public.

Power

In school administration, the struggle for power takes place within the corporate model adopted by educators in the early twentieth century. For example, the superintendent of a school district occupies the top position in the hierarchy, and orders flow from top to bottom. Standing between the superintendent and the schools is a central office staff, which supervises and monitors the flow of incoming and outgoing information.

Administrators in the central office are often in conflict with those in the field. Each claims that the other does not understand their problems. Field administrators, usually principals and assistant principals, feel that administrators in the central office, often referred to as "downtown," are out of touch with the real world of the schools and make demands that disrupt the enterprise of educating students. In response, central office staffers claim that they have to deal with the broad educational picture, which field administrators do not understand. The split between field and downtown administrators occurs in a similar form among local, state and federal education officials. Local school administrators accuse state authorities of being unaware of the real problems of the schools and of pursuing political objectives. On the other hand, state school officials are suspicious of local educators. Often, state officials believe that local school administrators sabotage state programs out of a lack of understanding and narrowness of vision.

Historically, the split between federal school authorities and local school districts has shaped the direction of federal aid to local schools. During the 1950s, local educators were accused by school critics of making the schools anti-intellectual, and because of this, of putting the country at a disadvantage in the Cold War with the Soviet Union. School critics opposed general aid to public schools because they believed local educators would misuse the funds. Consequently, the federal government adopted a policy of categorical aid, with the intention of forcing local schools to abide by federal educational policies. One result was that local school officials complained that politicians in Washington did not understand the real educational problems of those in the field.

Accompanying the tension between field administrators and central office personnel are turf battles and attempts to extend power. In a bureaucracy, the more responsibility a person has, the higher his or her status, power, and sometimes income. Bureaucrats resist surrendering functions to other parts of the organization, and seek to increase the importance of their role in the organization. Therefore, educational policies are often caught in the crossfire that occurs in territorial battles between field and downtown administrators, state and local administrators, and federal and state officials.

One method used by bureaucrats at all levels of government to deal with perceived incompetence or lack of understanding from another part of bureaucracy is to engage in *discretionary insubordination*. The phenomenon of discretionary insubordination is highlighted in a study of Chicago school principals. The authors of the study argue that as educational bureaucracies become larger, their members must often ignore the chain of command by disobeying or changing orders. Without discretionary insubordination, the researchers believe, the educational bureaucracy would not be able to adapt to human needs. They state that the object of discretionary disobedience "is to obey in such a way that the disobedient behavior produces the maximum effect locally—that is, within the school—but the minimum impact on one's superiors." [23]

One example of discretionary insubordination is the principal who must decide whether or not to meet a deadline for submitting paperwork to the central office. From the perspective of the school principal, the administrators downtown generate paperwork in their quest for something to do. Because much of the work is without immediate educational value and school principals risk being swamped in paper work from the central office, the viability of the system depends on lower-level administrators determining which paperwork is urgent and worthwhile.

While hierarchical organization, turf battles, splits between headquarters and field administrators, and discretionary insubordination characterize power politics within the educational bureaucracy, the desire to control defines the relationship between the educational bureaucracy and the community. In *School Politics Chicago Style*, Paul Peterson describes how Chicago school administrators resisted attempts to share power with the local community. In one situation described by Peterson, school administrators could not avoid meeting some of the demands for greater community participation in decision making in the school system. They responded by placing community advisory groups in the schools and turning over responsibility for their operation to school principals, thereby preserving their power. Peterson writes, with regard to the unwillingness of the bureaucracy to share power, "organizational resistance to sharing power with outsiders was increasingly successful the closer proposed changes approached real centers of power with the organization."[24]

The classic study of the desire by educational bureaucracies to maintain control has been written by Joseph McGivney and James Haught.[25] They found that actions by the central office staff could be best explained and predicted by the desire to control a situation. This most often occurs in relationships between the central office staff and the community. Central office administrators are often hostile to any public input into the school system that is not under the control of the informal network of the school bureaucracy. The general view of administrators is that most outsiders who want to make changes in the school system are troublemakers. In part, according to McGivney and Haught, the desire to control is a result of the desire to avoid any public criticism of members of the central office staff.

McGivney and Haught found that the organizational methods for maintaining control included control over the flow of information, the hiring of new personnel, and promotion from within the organization. The researchers found that informal networks within the central office staff must be satisfied in the decision-making process. Approval by these informal networks is required before any proposal originating outside the school bureaucracy is given serious consideration by the school system.

They also found that the effort to control public input depends on the amount of public criticism. The greater the public criticism of the school, the greater the desire by the central office to maintain control. In other words, the more the public demands control of the schools, the more the bureaucracy protects its power.

Educational administrators have resisted sharing power with the public and with teachers. Within the corporation-like school hierarchy, teachers are at the bottom of the chain of command and the objects of power from above. Teachers' unions have attempted to provide an antidote to the corporate model of school organization. Beginning in the 1970s, the *teacher power movement* has been an important element in the politics of education.

Two aspects of teacher power can be identified. The first is the direct involvement by teachers in politics as a means of insuring the passage of state and national laws that support their educational interests. A symbolic step in this direction was the 1976 endorsement of

Jimmy Carter for the presidency by the National Education Association. This was the first time the largest of the teachers' unions had endorsed a presidential candidate. Since the 1970s, both teachers' unions (the NEA and the AFT) have flexed their political muscle by supporting and campaigning for candidates for local, state, and national offices.

The second aspect of teacher power is the relationship of teachers to the rest of the educational bureaucracy. Currently, teachers find themselves in direct competition with administrators for control of educational policy. Teachers have strengthened their position within the educational system through contract agreements achieved through collective bargaining.

One issue in contract negotiations is control of working conditions. Teachers' unions, with varying success, have attempted to gain contract agreements on class size, the length of the working day, the number of meetings that can be called by the building principal, extracurricular assignments, and the teaching schedule. In addition, unions have sought control of teacher evaluations, textbook selections, and general educational policies.

Administrators and teachers' union will continue to compete for power over the educational system. Their battle will take place against a background of community attempts to participate in the control of school systems. Thus educational administrators will struggle to protect their power from other members of the bureaucracy, the public, and teachers' unions. It is also possible, given the nature of organizations, that as teachers gain power they will unite with administrators to resist public involvement in school governance.

Income

The pursuit of money is a major element in the internal politics of education. Administrators, teachers, and members of the knowledge industry vie for greater shares of the money spent on education. In his study of the central office staff of the Chicago public schools, Paul Petersosn found that educational bureaucrats are interested primarily in policies that increase the economic benefits of the members of their organization; policies in five major areas were found to enhance the position of bureaucrats:

1. Salaries
2. Increasing the number of jobs within the bureaucracy
3. Promotion from within the organization
4. Protecting the organization from outside interests
5. Increasing the prestige of the organization.[26]

Increasing the number of jobs in the educational bureaucracy and promoting from within the organization provide administrators with more opportunities to increase their salaries. Obviously, a greater number of jobs increases the chances for promotion to a higher-paying position. Limiting promotion to persons within the organization decreases competition for higher-paying jobs.

Items four and five reflect the desire of administrators to maintain control over outside influences and to increase the amount of money flowing into the educational enterprise. Obviously, the more money the school receives, the more likely it is that administrators' salaries will rise. Efforts to protect the organization and maintain its prestige can make the public more willing to spend money on schools.

Such policies often conflict with the economic goals of teachers. Teachers, like administrators, want increased salaries. From the perspective of teachers' unions, any increase in the size of the educational bureaucracy means a decrease in the money available for teachers' salaries. Therefore, in addition to their efforts to increase teacher power and control, the unions resist attempts to expand the educational bureaucracy. On the other hand, teachers join administrators in trying to win greater financial support for the schools. Teachers and administrators are quick to defend the public-school enterprise against outside criticism, but they disagree over how the money should be spent.

Over the last several decades, salary issues have been the primary cause of teacher strikes in the United States. In the 1960s, when teachers' unions conducted their first major strikes, wage issues involved a demand for a simple salary schedule that provided guaranteed annual increases and also pay increases for earning additional college credits.

In the 1980s negotiations over teachers' salaries were complicated by the introduction of career ladders and merit pay. First, unless career ladders or merit pay are mandated by the state, local unions must decide whether to accept or reject these new pay proposals. Second, if the unions accept either proposal, they have to bargain over the conditions surrounding each proposal. For instance, if a local teachers' union agrees to merit pay, then it has to negotiate the percentage of the salary increase that will be devoted to merit pay and the methods to be used for determining merit. If there is agreement over career ladders, then methods of promotion, the number of steps in the career ladder, and the salary increases attached to each step must be determined through collective bargaining. If state legislatures mandate career ladders, then teachers' unions must work at the state level to influence legislation regarding salaries and promotions.

While each change in the political climate of education provides new opportunities for profits by private companies, it also creates the possibility of political battles over limited educational funds. With all levels of government providing limited amounts of money for education, there always exists the potential for conflict over the percentage of the economic pie to be received by different sectors of the education world. If the amount of money for education is fixed, then any increase in spending for teachers' salaries, administrative salaries, or textbooks would result in reduced spending in other areas.

The same situation exists among education programs at different levels of government. For example, in 1986 the federal government proposed shifting funds from major education programs to a new antidrug campaign in the public schools. Because of the wide publicity given in 1986 to the cocaine-related deaths of two major sports stars, both political parties decided that a strong antidrug stance was good politics. But the Republican administration wanted to launch an antidrug program in the schools without increasing federal spending on education. The result, according to the *New York Times*, was that "Education Department officials ..., along with Republicans in Congress, ... said ... they would agree to finance the plan through cuts in other areas." The primary federal programs available for major cuts were student aid for higher education and aid to handicapped and disadvantaged children. On the other hand, Republicans admitted that they hoped to be relieved of the political burden of making cuts in education programs for the drug legislation by letting the Democrats vote money for the antidrug campaign.[27]

Changes like those described above can result in major shifts in income within the education world. Obviously, a national antidrug program would allow publishers to increase their profits by producing materials on drug abuse for use in the public schools. Experts on substance abuse could gather more fees by conducting staff development programs in the schools. University-based researchers would also find a new source of funds. In other words, changes in educational policies directly affect the distribution of money in the knowledge industry.

Even competition between differing research paradigms can affect the flow of money. During the 1960s and early 1970s, research money from the government and foundations went primarily to research projects that had a strong quantitative orientation. This trend changed in the late 1970s with the increasing popularity of qualitative, or ethnographic, research. The present result is competition between quantitative and qualitative researchers for limited educational funds.

In conclusion, important political conflicts occur within the education establishment over the distribution of education funds. It could be hypothesized that conflict over money increases as the availability of education funds decreases. On the other hand, it could also be hypothesized that conflict over money exists even with a surplus of education funds, because educators and members of the knowledge industry can always find new ways of spending increasing amounts of money.

CONCLUSION

Political conflict over government-operated schools is inevitable in a heterogeneous society like that in the United States. In a multicultural society, disagreements exist about moral values, religious doctrines, political ideas, and cultural beliefs. The common-school ideal of eliminating cultural differences by teaching a consensus of values and beliefs proved unworkable because of the political conflict over the values and beliefs that were to form the public-school consensus.

Political conflict is also generated when schools are used to enhance economic opportunities and increase political power. Politicians compete with each other for political positions, and workers and businesspeople compete for higher wages and profits. Schools supply the arena for such competition. Differing political groups each want their ideas emphasized in the schools. Politicians attempt to win votes by claiming that their educational policies will improve schools and society. Ethnic politicians demand language and cultural policies in schools that maintain the cohesiveness of their particular constituencies. And a long-standing conflict has existed between business interests and workers over the content of education. Many workers want schools to be avenues of economic mobility for their children, while many businesspeople want the schools to focus on job training to meet corporate needs.

In addition, there is continual political conflict over the funding of education and the distribution of educational monies. Most people want to minimize their tax burden and increase their government benefits. Interest groups continue to struggle over who should pay most of the taxes to support education. At the same time, interest groups continue to battle over the distribution of educational funds. The major political issues in school finance are inequality in the distribution of government money, attempts to increase educational choice by direct or indirect funding of private education, and the sharing of the tax burden.

These inherent political conflicts in education contribute to the dynamic of change discussed in Chapter 1. The pursuit of both self-interest and educational ideals by elected politicians, educational politicians, interest groups, and the knowledge industry—combined with political conflict over language, religion, culture, political ideas, economic goals, and school funding—creates constant tension in the educational system. Adding to this dynamic quality of American schooling is the pursuit within the educational establishment of increased power and money. Given the importance of ideas in a democratic society, one might conclude that the school—as a major distributor to young people of ideas, values, and status—will inevitably be caught in a complex web of political conflict.

NOTES

1. Stanley Aronowitz and Henry Giroux, *Education under Siege: The Conservative, Liberal, and Radical Debate over Schooling* (South Hadley, Mass.: Bergin & Garvey, 1985), pp. 69–115.
2. Martin Carnoy, *Education as Cultural Imperialism* (White Plains, N.Y. Longman, 1974).
3. John N. Hawkins, "The People's Republic of China: Educational Policy and National Minorities—The Politics of Intergroup Relations" in R. Murray Thomas, ed., *Politics and Education: Cases from Eleven Nations* (New York: Pergamon Press, 1983), pp. 125–149.
4. Richard Manning, "Soweto—The Spirit of '76: Three Black Leaders Recall a Day of Glory and a Decade of Disunity," *Newsweek*, (June 23, 1986), pp. 40–42.
5. James Crawford, "Bilingual Educators Seeking Strategies to Counter Attacks." *Education Week*, Vol. 5, No. 28 (April 9, 1986), 1, 9.
6. James Crawford, "Adminstration Panel Praises Bennett's Bilingual-Education Stance," *Education Week*, Vol. 5, No. 28 (April 9, 1986), p. 9.
7. R. Ben-Chaim, "America in the Mind of Israel," *New York Times Magazine* (June 29, 1986), p. 58.
8. Carl Kaestle, *Pillars of the Republic: Common Schools and American Society* (New York: Hill and Wang, 1983).
9. For a discussion of the Supreme Court rulings regarding education and religion, see Joel Spring, *American Education*, 3rd ed. (White Plains, N.Y.: Longman, 1985), pp. 23–48.
10. William J. Reese, "Soldiers for Christ in the Army of God: The Christian School Movement in America," *Educational Theory*, Vol. 35, No. 2 (Spring 1985), 175–194.
11. An early expression of this issue in the black community can be found in W. E. B. DuBois, "The Souls of Black Folk," in John Hope Franklin, ed., *Three Negro Classics* (New York: Avon Books, 1965).
12. Lawrence Cremin, ed., *The Republic and the School: Horace Mann on the Education of Free Men* (New York: Teachers College Press, 1957), pp. 94–97.

13. The best examples of the debate are Booker T. Washington's "Up from Slavery" and W. E. B. DuBois's "The Souls of Black Folk," in Franklin, ed., *Three Negro Classics*.
14. Mortimer J. Adler, *The Paideia Proposal* (New York: Macillan, 1982).
15. See William Russell, *Education and the Working Class: The Expansion of Public Education during the Transition to Capitalism*, Ph.D. dissertation, University of Cincinnati, 1981.
16. See Henry Allen Bullock, *A History of Negro Education in the South: From 1619 to the Present* (New York: Praeger, 1970).
17. Washington, "Up from Slavery" and DuBois, "The Souls of Black Folk."
18. See Joel Spring, *The American School: 1642–1985* (White Plains: Longman, 1986), pp. 88–89.
19. Ira Shore, *Culture Wars: School and Society in the Conservative Restoration, 1969–1984* (Boston: Routledge & Kegan Paul, 1986), p. 152.
20. Ibid., p. 152.
21. See Joel Spring, "Political and Economic Analysis" in Philip Altabach, Gail Kelly, and Lois Weis, eds., *Excellence in Education: Perspectives on Policy and Practice* (Buffalo: Prometheus Books, 1985), pp. 75–91.
22. Shor, *Cultural Wars*, p. 153.
23. Quoted in Kathryn Borman and Joel Spring, *Schools in Central Cities* (White Plains, N.Y. Longman, 1984), p. 97.
24. Paul E. Peterson, *School Politics Chicago Style* (Chicago: University of Chicago Press, 1976), p. 93.
25. Joseph McGivney and James Haught, "The Politics of Education: A View from the Perspective of the Central Office Staff," *Educational Administration Quarterly* Vol. 8 (Autunm 1972), 18– .
26. Peterson, *School Politics*, p. 112.
27. *New York Times* (August 12, 1986), Section A, p. 19.

CHAPTER 3

Policy and Implementation in the Federal Government

For the purpose of national-level analysis, a distinction will be made between the politics of policy and the politics of implementation. The *politics of policy* refers to the struggles between interest groups and politicians that result in the formulation of national educational policy. On the other hand, the *politics of implementation* involves the struggles between politicians, interest groups, and bureaucrats over the implementation of policy.

These two analytical categories, as indicated in Table 3.1, can be divided according to the origins of political action. For instance, federal policy can originate from grass roots movements that pressure politicians to enact legislation. The civil rights movement and the campaign for educational rights for the handicapped are good examples of grass roots movements that have produced federal educational legislation. In some situations, politicians advocate educational policies in order to win votes and build a constituency. In 1980, the Republican party organized a constituency of private-school supporters and religious reformers around educational policies that included tuition tax credits, school prayer, and abolishing the Department of Education. Educational policy also originates in debates about other national problems. Historically, concern with national defense and the economy has resulted in a variety of federal educational legislation.

The responses of politicians to voters are part of the politics of implementation. In the 1980s, Republicans promised voters less federal regulation and intrusion into state and local governments. These campaign promises were actualized in deregulation, and by the shifting of part of the control over federal programs to state and local school

TABLE 3.1 POLITICS OF POLICY AND IMPLEMENTATION

Origins of Federal Educational Policy
Grass roots movements
Political strategy
National policy concerns

Causes of Struggles over Implementation
Bureaucratic conflict
Political strategy and interest groups

authorities. In addition, struggles occur between bureaucrats at different levels over the control of federal programs. For instance, local school authorities often object to the authority of state educational agencies.

Like many categories used in this analysis, those in Table 3.1 are interconnected and overlapping. Grass roots movements catch the eye of politicians, who see another source of votes. Concerns with unemployment or defense are quickly translated by politicians into proposals for more and better education. Local school authorities pressure their political representatives to free them from federal paperwork and red tape.

Not only are the origins of policy and the politics of implementation interconnected, federal educational policies and actions are closely intertwined with state and local governments. The implementation of most federal education programs requires the cooperation of state and local school authorities. In many cases, federal programs create new state and local bureaucratic structures.

The following sections on federal policy and implementation illustrate an interesting case in the politics of research. The bulk of recent research deals with the politics of implementation.[1] A major reason for this is that federally supported research does not focus on why particular educational policies develop. Obviously, a Democratic or Republican administration is not interested in supporting research that examines the political forces that shape the educational policies of its party. Such research might result in public disclosures that would be embarrassing to the party. Consequently, federally supported policy research lacks a critical edge and does not deal with the structure of power. Given the fact that most scholars dealing with policy issues depend on government grants, most policy research tends to serve power rather than analyze it.

GRASS ROOTS MOVEMENTS

Two major grass roots movements, the civil rights movement and the handicapped rights movement, show one cause of federal involvement in education. In both cases, the lack of response from state and local governments forced each movement to turn to the courts and the federal government. Both political movements eventually established an iron triangle between government agencies and politicians.

The civil rights movement dates back to the nineteenth century, when Southern states passed laws requiring segregation in education, public accommodations, transportation, and other public facilities. The black community, disenfranchised by Southern voting laws, was unable to exert political power at the local level to end school segregation. Consequently, black organizations, led by the NAACP, carried their battle into the courts and successfully achieved school desegregation with the 1954 U.S. Supreme Court decision, *Brown v. Board of Education.*

The Brown decision, along with its implementation decision in 1955, could not, however, force the Southern school systems into desegregating. The civil rights movement had to pressure the federal government. In addition, it had to resort to nonviolent sit-downs and demonstrations to force the desegregation of public facilities and transportation. A variety of civil rights organizations were formed, including the Congress on Racial Equality and the Student Nonviolent Coordinating Committee. The most important of these organizations was the Southern Christian Leadership Conference under the direction of Martin Luther King, Jr.

In the 1950s and early 1960s, desegregation struggles literally took place in the streets. Liberal political leaders in the Democratic party responded to the growing unrest by proposing a series of Civil Rights acts, the most important of which was passed in 1964. The 1964 Civil Rights Act gave teeth to federal desegregation efforts by decreeing that federal monies would be withheld from institutions that discriminated according to race, religion, or ethnic origin. This legislation established the precedent of policing institutions that received federal monies for civil rights violations, including, eventually, discrimination based on gender and handicaps.

To be an effective weapon against school segregation, the 1964 Civil Rights Act required major federal funding of education. This funding came in 1965 with passage of the Elementary and Secondary Education Act (ESEA), which contained Title I (now called Chapter 1), supporting compensatory education. ESEA was part of the War on

Poverty conducted by the federal government in the 1960s.

During the administrations of presidents John F. Kennedy and Lyndon B. Johnson, ESEA was one response to the civil rights movement and a growing national concern with poverty. In the early 1960s, Martin Luther King, Jr., shifted the emphasis of the civil rights movement to a poor people's campaign to eradicate poverty in the United States. The Democratic party, which, during the New Deal years of the Depression, had structured its voter support around the poor, organized labor, urban blue-collar workers, Catholics, and minority groups, responded to the rising tide of protest from minority groups and the poor.

The problem facing President Kennedy's administration in the early 1960s was to draft educational legislation that was responsive to the poor and civil rights groups, and, at the same time, balance the interests of the various constituencies in the party. Of particular importance were Catholic school leaders who wanted to receive some benefit from any federal education legislation.[2]

In addition, education lobbyists feuded over whether to emphasize funding elementary and secondary education or higher education. President Kennedy's commissioner of education, Francis Keppel, recalled the antagonism that existed in 1962 between the education lobbyists, "It was obvious that the best hope that one could have would be to keep a program before the Congress ... and try to keep the lobbyists from killing each other, oh, because the higher education fellows were so mad at the NEA fellows they wouldn't speak to them."[3]

While education lobbyists bickered with each other over the emphasis in federal legislation, they were united in opposition to aid to religious schools. For instance, Edgar Fuller, executive secretary of the Council of Chief State School Officers, testified before Congress in 1962 on behalf of the American Association of School Administrators, the American Vocational Association, the National Congress of Parents and Teachers, the National School Boards Association, and his own organization against aid to sectarian schools. He argued that it was unwise public policy and would result in educational legislation being declared unconstitutional.[4]

After President Kennedy's assassination, President Johnson decided to overcome religious conflicts and squabbles between education lobbyists by linking educational legislation to his War on Poverty. In addition, Johnson developed a strategy for overcoming fears about federal control of education. In his study of education legislation during the Kennedy and Johnson years, Hugh Davis describes the problem for the Johnson administration, "The best way to avoid the charge of federal control was to provide general aid to the states in the form of what the Bureau of the Budget abhorred as the leave-it-on-the-stump-and-run variety." But, according to Davis, "if this aid was to be for public schools only, so as to keep church and state separate, it of course aroused the intense opposition of the Roman Catholic lobby and thereby split the Democratic constituency." [5]

The problem was resolved in a brilliant stroke of political strategy. The strategic thinking on the issue is contained in a memo written in 1964 by Commissioner of Education Francis Keppel. Keppel outlined three legislative options. This first was to provide general aid to public schools. This, he argued, would cause a negative reaction from Catholic groups and spark a battle between Catholics, on one side, and the NEA and the Council of Chief State School Officer, on the other. The second option was to provide general aid to both public and private schools. This, he predicted, would cause a strong reaction from the NEA and would split the Democratic party, since Southern Democrats objected to any aid to Catholic schools. In addition, there was the issue of the constitutionality of federal aid to religious schools.

The third option, and the one that eventually became the Elementary and Secondary Education Act of 1965, was to drop the idea of general aid and focus on educational aid to the children of the poor. From Keppel's perspective, most education lobbyists would support the proposal and many Southern Democrats would back it because they represented depressed rural areas. Catholic schools could be included because the money would go to benefit poor children and not religious institutions. In addition, in response to charges of federal control, the legislation would provide money to strengthen and expand state departments of education so that they could administer the legislation. [6]

This political strategy produced one of the most important pieces of federal education legislation in modern times. It had major consequences for future federal legislative action. First, it signaled the abandonment of general federal aid to education in favor of categorical aid. One consequence was to tie federal aid to other national policy concerns such as poverty, defense, and economic growth. Second, it solved the religious issue by linking federal aid to educational programs that could be used in parochial schools to benefit children and not religion. However, this would remain a constitutional issue as the courts continually refined the extent of federal involvement in religious schools. And last, to avoid charges of federal control, the reliance on state departments of education to administer federal funds resulted in an expansion of those bureaucracies and a much larger role for state government in local education. This trend accelerated in the 1980s, when, in an attempt to reduce federal control, the Reagan administration consolidated educational legislation into block grants to be planned and administered at the state and local levels.

The political movement for federal legislation to aid the handicapped followed a path similar to the civil rights movement. First, finding themselves unable to change educational institutions by pressuring local and state governments, organized groups interested in improving educational opportunities for the handicapped turned to the courts. This was the path taken in the late 1960s by the Pennsylvania Association for Retarded Children (PARC).

PARC was one of many associations organized in the 1950s to aid handicapped and retarded citizens. These organizations were concerned with state laws that excluded retarded and handicapped citizens from educational institutions because they were considered ineducable and untrainable. State organizations like PARC and the National Association for Retarded Children campaigned to eliminate these laws and to demonstrate the educability of all children. But, as the civil rights movement discovered throughout the century, local and state officials were resistant to change and relief had to be sought from the judicial system.

In *Pennsylvania Association for Retarded Children [PARC] v. Commonwealth of Pennsylvania*, a case that was as important to the handicapped rights movement as the *Brown* decision was to the civil rights movement, PARC objected to conditions in the Pennhurst State School and Hospital. In framing the case, lawyers for PARC focused on the legal right to an education for handicapped and retarded children. PARC, working with the major federal lobbyist for handicapped children, the Council for Exceptional Children (CEC), overwhelmed the court with evidence on the educability of handicapped and retarded children. The state withdrew its case, and the court enjoined the state from excluding mentally retarded children from a public education and required that every mentally retarded child be allowed access to an education.[7]

Publicity about the PARC case prompted lobbying groups representing the handicapped to file thirty-six cases against state governments. The CEC prepared model legislation and lobbied for its passage at the state and federal levels.

Unlike the political struggle over the 1965 ESEA, advocates of federal legislation for the handicapped and retarded did not have problems with religious conflicts. On the other hand, there was the possibility of excessive federal control resulting from attempts to define for each handicapped or retarded child an appropriate education. In fact, to do so would have raised the specter of federal control of local education and alienated many members of Congress.

The resolution of this political problem, as it appeared in 1975 in Public Law 94–142 (Education for All Handicapped Children Act), was the requirement that an individual educational plan (IEP) be developed for each child jointly by the local educational agency and the child's parents or guardians. This gives the child or the parents the right to negotiate with the local school system about the type of services to be delivered.

The IEP was considered to be a brilliant political strategy. In their study of the legalization of special education, David Neal and David Kirp call the IEP "an ingenious device in terms of political acceptability." They write,

> It avoids attempting to mandate specific services; it recognizes the rights of recipients, empowers them, and involves them in the process; it avoids treading on the professional discretion of teachers and potentially enhances their influence over placement decisions; it provides a means of holding local administrators accountable while paying some deference to the belief that the federal government should not interfere too much with local autonomy in education; and it appeals to local school officials by fixing the upper limit of the liabilities with respect to the child.[8]

The civil rights movement and the struggle for handicapped rights resulted in federal educational legislation and the establishment of iron triangles between lobbyists, politicians, and federal administrators. In the previously mentioned study of federal education policy in the Kennedy and Johnson administrations, Hugh Graham argues that federal education programs survived the transition in 1968 from a Democratic to a Republic administration because the "overlapping educational constituencies had by the late 1960s formed their iron-triangle relationships with congressional subcommittees and the executive agencies . . . and proposals for renewal . . . went crunching through the congressional machinery. . . ."[9]

In *The Troubled Crusade: American Education 1945–1980*, historian Diane Ravitch describes the iron triangle formed around education for the handicapped. According to her, handicapped interest groups "forged close relationships . . . with the staff and members of the congressional education committees and with the federal agency officers responsible for administering programs for the handicapped." In describing the iron triangle, she states, "Congressional staff worked with the representatives of the handicapped to develop new legislation, BEH [Bureau of Education for the Handicapped] urged stronger enforcement and more funds, and spokesmen [sic] for the interest groups were well prepared whenever hearings were called or when new regulations were being drafted." [10]

In summary, the pattern for federal involvement in education as a result of grass roots movements is the following:

1. A grass roots movement is unable to affect change at the local and state level.
2. The grass roots movement seeks the aid of court system.
3. Finding resolution of problem too slow after winning court battle, the grass roots movement seeks federal legislation.
4. Attempts to achieve federal legislation require political strategies that influence the content of the legislation (e.g., categorical aid, support of state educational agencies, and IEP);
5. Political efforts at federal level result in the forging of an iron triangle between the interest group, federal agencies, and politicians.

POLITICAL STRATEGY

As mentioned at the beginning of this chapter, there is a thin line between federal educational policies brought about by pressure from grass roots movements and policies initiated by politicians to win votes. Often, it is hard to determine original causes and effects. While it is difficult to make a clear distinction between causal factors, it is possible to point to situations in which politicians have acted consciously to organize and please an educational constituency. In these situations, federal policy has been linked directly to political strategy.

For instance, consider the political strategy in President Ronald Reagan's appointment of educational politician William Bennett as secretary of education in 1985. During the 1980 presidential campaign, the Republican party formed its educational constituency around interest groups concerned with private schooling, school prayer, and moral values in the curriculum. On the other side of the fence, Democrats were supported by organized educational interests, including the NEA and AFT.

The most prominent religious and conservative groups forming the educational constituency of the Republican party were the Moral Majority, the Heritage Foundation, and Phyllis Schlafly's Eagle Forum. These conservative organizations, along with other organizations, formed a coalition under an umbrella organization called the Committee for the Survival of a Free Congress.

These conservative organizations, and other conservative appointees to the Department of Education, complained that Terrel Bell, President Reagan's first secretary of education, was being unduly influenced by the education community. For instance, during the early years of the Reagan administration, conservatives within the Department of Education drafted regulations to provide stiffer enforcement of the Hatch Amendment. The Hatch Amendment was passed in 1978 but remained unenforced until the Reagan administration. The amendment required parental approval before any child in a public school could be given psychiatric, psychological, or behavioral testing or questioning. Conservatives believed the amendment provided protection against public-school meddling in student values. Based on the Hatch Amendment, Phyllis Schlafly's Eagle Forum issued a form letter to parents in which they could advise their local school districts that they did not want their children to be involved in any psychiatric, psychological, or behavioral questioning or testing. The form letter objected to school activities such as values clarification, death education, discussion and testing of interpersonal relations, sex education, drug and alcohol education, and "anti-nationalistic, one-world government, or globalism curricula." [11]

Conservative appointees within the Department of Education complained when Secretary Bell dragged his feet on enforcing the provisions of the Hatch Amendment. Charlotte Iserbyt, an employee of the Department of Education, wrote in a memorandum to other conservatives that, "Bell doesn't like them [the Hatch Amendment regulations], and he does not want to offend his educationist friends by signing off on regulations that will disturb their *modus operandi....*" Iserbyt believed that educators were trying to change "the values, attitudes, and beliefs of students to conform with those necessary to bring about a socialist/humanist one-world government." [12]

Conservatives were therefore pleased when Bell resigned in 1985 and Reagan appointed William Bennett. Reagan failed to accomplish his campaign promises to abolish the Department of Education and gain passage of a school prayer amendment and tuition tax credit legislation. Bennett's appointment was an attempt to hold the Republican educational constituency together and silence conservative critics.

With the appointment of Bennett, the Moral Majority report of 1985 proudly announced in headlines, "Finally a Friend in Education." [13] The Moral Majority has steadily gained strength within the Department of Education. For instance, in 1985, Thomas Tancredo, the Department of Education's Region VIII representative in Denver, distributed at government expense a speech written five years previously by the then executive director of the Moral Majority, Robert

Billings. The speech declared that "godlessness has taken over America." President Reagan appointed Billings to direct the Department of Education's ten regional offices.[14]

During confirmation hearings before the Senate Committee on Labor and Human Resources, Bennett, under oath, admitted that he had been screened for the position of secretary of education by twelve conservative organizations meeting under the umbrella of the Committee for the Survival of a Free Congress. He claimed that he was forced to attend that meeting by pressure from the White House. Bennett told the Senate committee that he received a call from Ms. Lynn Ross Wood of the Office of Presidential Personnel. "The advice to me," he said, "was to attend the meeting, that they requested that I should attend this meeting."[15]

President Reagan's appointment of William Bennett introduced a particular leadership style and educational philosophy to the Department of Education. Bennett announced that he was going to use the office as a "bully pulpit" to influence educational policy through rhetoric and pronouncements. In addition, Bennett championed a core curriculum emphasizing the humanities in the context of Western civilization—a curriculum that ignored the culture of many of the ethnic groups supporting the Democratic party. This political bias was evident in a statement to the Senate confirmation hearings by Arnoldo S. Torres, national executive director of the League of United Latin American Citizens (LULAC). In reference to Bennett's emphasis on Western civilization in the core curriculum, Torres stated: "Yet Western Europe is merely one continent on the globe; the melting pot of North America also has its roots in the cultures of the East, of Africa, of the Pacific, and finally of the rest of the Western Hemisphere—Central and Latin America."[16]

The appointment of educational politicians like Bennett can result in an emphasis on particular federal educational policies. Politicians consciously trying to gain votes can also create support for particular educational policies. In the previously cited study of federal education policy in the Kennedy and Johnson years, Hugh Graham provides the example of liberal Democratic Senator Ralph Yarborough of Texas who, believing that he would lose the 1970 election to a wealthy and conservative Democrat, decided that Hispanic support was crucial for his coalition of blacks, Mexican-Americans, and poor whites.[17]

In an effort to win Hispanic support, Yarborough, after getting appointed to a special subcommittee on bilingual education of the Senate Committee on Labor and Public Welfare, launched a series of hearings in major Hispanic communities. Ethnic political lobbyists, and not educational experts or linguistic theorists, gave most of the testimony. The hearings concluded in East Harlem, with Senator Kennedy and the Bronx Borough President Herman Badillo decrying the fact that there were no Puerto Rican principals and only a few Puerto Rican teachers in the New York City school system.[18]

Yarborough supported bilingual legislation that focused on students whose "mother tongue is Spanish." The legislation included programs to impart knowledge and pride about Hispanic culture and language, and to bring descendants of Mexicans and Puerto Ricans into the teaching profession. The legislation was clearly designed to win political support from the Hispanic community.

The opportunistic nature of Yarborough's legislation was highlighted in Congressional hearings when Commissioner of Education Harold Howe pointed out that bilingual education programs were already being funded to the level of $13 million under Title I of the 1965 ESEA and that Yarborough's bill provided only $10 million. In addition, the needs of other children such as those of Korean or Chinese descent were ignored in the legislation. In Graham's words, "Senator Yarborough was not primarily interested in the bloc vote of Korean Texans."[19]

The Johnson administration opposed a separate bilingual education bill because of the programs developed under ESEA and the explicit Hispanic bias of the proposed legislation. But in the end, according to Graham, the political arguments won out. The administration compromised by supporting the legislation, and Congress compromised by removing the Hispanic bias. The result was separate legislation for bilingual education. As an ironic comment on the political value of educational issues, Yarborough lost the 1970 Democratic primary to Houston millionaire Lloyd Benson.

The above examples illustrate the kind of federal policy that is produced when politicians and educational politicians use educational issues to win votes. In one case, the goal was to respond to criticism from educational supporters and, in the other, the goal was to gain supporters. The political strategies included appointment of particular educational politicians and the support of particular legislation. In each case, political strategies committed the federal government to a set of educational policies.

NATIONAL POLICY

National political, social, and economic issues are a major source of change in federal educational policy. In response to national issues, the schools often become both scapegoats and citadels of hope. For instance, in the Cold War years of the 1950s, the schools were criticized for being the weakest link in national defense. One aspect of the arms race was the competition between U.S. and Soviet schools to educate the best scientists, mathematicians, and engineers. One result of the Cold War was the 1958 National Defense Education Act, which supported math, science, and foreign language programs in the public schools. In the 1960s, national concerns focused on the issue of poverty, and the schools were blamed for being racist institutions and perpetuators of poverty. Within this climate, the already-discussed ESEA was passed in 1965. In the 1980s the schools have been blamed for not preparing students to help America compete in international markets against the Japanese and West Germans.

Educational interest groups tend to jump on the bandwagon with each new shift in national policy concerns. For example, the "Sony War" of the 1980s turned federal educational policy around and caused a struggle between educational interest groups for a share of the federal budget pie. The battle cry of the Sony War in education was given in 1983 by the National Commission on Excellence in Education when it declared in its report, A Nation at Risk, "Our nation is at risk. Our once-unchallenged preeminence in commerce, industry, science, and technological innovation is being overtaken by competitors throughout the world." The report placed the blame on the schools with the warning, "the educational foundations of our society are presently being eroded by a rising tide of mediocrity that threatens our very future as a nation and a people." The report specifically warns of Japan's efficient automobile manufacturing, South Korea's steel production, and West German products.[20]

A Nation at Risk was issued after a period in the 1970s and early 1980s of relatively high unemployment, particularly among youth, declining productivity, and dwindling capital investment by American industry. In part, this high unemployment was caused by the large number of youth from the baby boom generation entering the labor market combined with a slow increase in the number of jobs. The result was a decline in wages, particularly for entry-level occupations, and a tendency by American business to limit capital investment and rely on inexpensive labor. The resulting decrease in capital investment caused a slow growth in productivity in American industry. Between 1960 and 1978, the average annual rate of increase in labor productivity in the United States was 1.7 percent; in Japan by contrast, it was 7.5 percent.[21]

Therefore the claim by A Nation at Risk, and by other educational reports in the early 1980s, that the poor academic quality of schools was responsible for the slow growth in the nation's productivity was inaccurate. The cause was to be found in decisions made by business management. In fact, it takes twenty years for a high school graduate to have an effect on the economy. A poorly educated high school graduate does not walk out of school and immediately bring down the economy. If one is going to blame the schools for the economic problems of the 1980s, then one has to blame the schools of the 1950s and early 1960s, not the schools of the 1970s.[22]

Clearly, most education reports in the early 1980s were using the public schools as a scapegoat for economic problems caused by factors outside the realm of education. But, against the background of these general economic concerns, there has emerged a school reform movement that emphasizes the teaching of traditional academic subjects, increasing the quality and number of science and mathematics courses, and changing the career structure of teachers.

The Reagan administration, which pledged to reduce federal involvement in education, has focused on improving the quality of teachers through merit pay. Of course, this has shifted the responsibility for action from the federal government to state and local school systems. In general, as will be discussed in Chapter 4 on state government, the educational reforms of the Sony War have been played out at the state level, with Secretary of Education William Bennett using his position as a "bully pulpit" to urge on the troops.

The Sony War has sparked one piece of federal legislation, the Education for Economic Security Act, which shows how educational interest groups respond to changing national policy issues. The purpose of the legislation was to provide money to strengthen education in mathematics, science, computer education, and foreign languages. Senator Robert Stafford opened the hearings with an ominous warning about educational conditions "which impede America's economic growth and undermine our national security."[23]

The two teachers' unions and the American Educational Research Association (AERA) were represented at the hearings, respectively, by William McGuire of the NEA, Albert Shanker of the AFT, and Patricia Graham, dean of the Harvard Graduate School of Education. Each spokesperson tried to persuade the senators to write legislation to reflect the interests of their particular organizations.

William McGuire, president of the NEA, argued that any aid should go directly to local school systems and avoid the state educational bureaucracy. From the standpoint of collective bargaining and teacher power, greater control over the funds could be exerted by teachers at the local level, as opposed to administrators at the state level. In the interest of teacher control and the NEA concept of professionalism, McGuire urged that the actual programs funded by the act be developed by local teachers working in cooperation with business and labor leaders. In addition, McGuire, in support of the NEA concept of a democratic pay scale, argued against higher pay for math, science, and foreign language teachers.[24]

The most self-serving aspect of the McGuire's testimony was his advocacy of NEA-proposed legislation, the American Defense Education Act (ADEA). The ADEA was an attempt by the NEA to use current concerns with the economy and defense to increase funding for education. The ADEA proposed a national program, administered at the local level, to improve instruction in math, science, and other subjects. In addition—and this represented the more sinister and self-serving qualities of the legislation—the ADEA proposed that the Department of Defense work closely with the public schools to insure that students would be educated to meet the personnel and educational needs of the military establishment. Thus the NEA jumped on the bandwagon of concern with international trade and defense and asked for more federal money to be controlled by teachers at the local level.[25]

The testimony of Albert Shanker, president of the AFT, was concerned with the needs of urban school teachers, who make up the bulk of the AFT's membership. A major problem that faced teachers during the 1970s was reductions in the work force caused by declining student enrollments. To aid laid-off teachers, the AFT bargained with school districts for retraining programs. These agreements were designed to protect the membership of the union and provide continued support for its leadership by insuring that older union members would remain in the school system.

Therefore, Shanker urged that the proposed legislation be written to retrain elementary and high school teachers to be effective math, science, and foreign language teachers. He singled out English and social studies teachers, who were in the greatest surplus and faced the worst employment difficulties, for retraining. This type of legislation would guarantee retention of union membership. It had the assured support of union leaders and was a better alternative than hiring younger teachers who would not be as committed to the union.[26]

Patricia Graham presented an entirely different agenda. Graham is a master educational politician who rose from the ranks of the faculty at Teachers College, Columbia University, in the 1970s to head the National Institute of Education (NIE). From the NIE, in a pattern followed by many educational politicians, she moved from the world of government to the ranks of educational administrators as dean of the Harvard Graduate School of Education.

Appearing before the Senate committee, Graham represented the AERA, whose membership includes most of the educational researchers in the United States. Obviously, Graham wanted to assure a steady flow of federal research money to the membership of the AERA and to the faculty of the Harvard Graduate School of Education. She argued before the committee, therefore, that improved instruction in science and mathematics depended on better educational research. Graham proceeded to list research needs that covered most of the research areas in AERA. She called for more federal research money for the development of instructional materials, the study of the effects of school organization on learning, the study of student achievement, and the study of how local and institutional policies affect the recruitment of teachers.[27]

At end of the testimony by the representatives of these three educational interest groups, Senator Edward Kennedy of Massachusetts asked them to identify, out of all the proposals being considered by the committee, the most important that the committee should consider. Without hesitating, Albert Shanker identified retraining teachers, William McGuire chose the American Defense Education Act, and Patricia Graham said the funding of educational research.[28]

The cacophony of interests presented at the Senate hearings exemplifies the tendency of educational interest groups to jump on the bandwagon created by national policy concerns. The Sony War sparked criticism of the schools and demands for educational change. Educational researchers, as represented by Patricia Graham and the AERA, predictably urged more money for educational research to solve national problems. The AFT rushed in with proposals to win the battle and maintain its rank-and-file support. And the NEA saw it as a golden opportunity for more federal money for education (to be controlled by teachers at the local level) and was willing to join ranks with the Department of Defense to gain that support.

The actions of educational interest groups reinforce a pattern of using the schools as scapegoats and as questionable instruments of policy. Rather than defend the schools against charges of destroying the economy and question claims that school reform will save America's position in world trade, educational groups seized the opportunity to ask for more money and protection of their interests. The pursuit of self-interest perpetuates the cycle of constant change in school policy with every shift in national policy.

THE POLITICS OF IMPLEMENTATION: BUREAUCRATIC STRUGGLE

The implementation of federal legislation often brings about political struggles between different levels of the educational bureaucracy. State education agencies and local school districts have always complained about federal red tape and regulations. In addition, local school districts have complained about the heavy hand of state government. For their part, Federal and state administrators have claimed that, without their respective guidance, the goals of federal legislation would not be achieved.

Paul Peterson and Barry Rabe have outlined the relationships that develop between the different levels of government with the implementation of federal legislation.[29] Eventually, they conclude, the struggle over the implementation of federal legislation is resolved with a cooperative relationship between new bureaucratic structures and professionals. But before this occurs, there are several stages of development.

In Stage One, according to Peterson and Rabe, Congress passes legislation with imprecise guidance on its implementation. This was the situation with the compensatory education programs of the 1965 ESEA. The legislation contained only a vague framework for creating compensatory education programs. In addition, no professional at the local school district level were prepared to deal with the new federal programs.

Federal regulations during the early years of ESEA were minimal and in some cases nonexistent. Consequently, local school districts organized their own programs without much intrusion from state and federal officials. In fact, state and federal governments lacked the staff to supervise the spending of federal money. For instance, in 1976, 14,000 school districts spent $120 million for compensatory education. At the same time, there were only 100 Office of Education staff members to supervise compensatory education programs. As a result, complaints were made that local school districts were improperly using federal money designated for compensatory education programs.[30]

In response to these complaints, federal control moved into what Peterson and Rabe designate as Stage Two. During this stage, the federal government attempts to control the actions of local school districts by drafting more specific guidelines and regulations. Interest groups also begin to exert influence over any amendments to the original law and over the regulations. In the case of compensatory education, these interest groups included the National Advisory Council for the Education of Disadvantaged Children, the Lawyers' Committee for Civil Rights under Law, the Legal Standards and Education Project of the NAACP, and the National Welfare Rights Organization. These groups demanded more specificity in federal regulations to correct what they believed to be the failure of local school systems to properly implement compensatory education programs.

Stage Three results, according to Peterson and Rabe, from complaints about federal red tape and control, and repeated conflicts between federal bureaucrats and local leaders over guidelines and expectations. Federal control begins to loosen, but it does not return to the conditions that existed under Stage One. Instead, the administration of federal programs at state and local levels is now in the hands of experienced professionals who understand and conform to the objectives of federal legislation. For instance, with regard to compensatory education programs, Peterson and Rabe write: "State-based professionals became increasingly aware of what was and was not expected by the federal government, as well as what was and was not feasible locally."[31] These state-based professionals, they argue, take pride in enforcing federal requirements.

Therefore, according to Peterson and Rabe, cooperation develops between local, state, and federal administrative structures. This cooperation is established between a new set of bureaucrats at each government level whose primary purpose is to deal with particular federal programs. It is not necessary, they argue, for every federal program to go through each evolutionary stage. For instance, federal programs for the handicapped were launched under the stringent controls of Stage Two. But eventually there developed a new cadre of professionals at the state and local level, and handicapped programs moved to Stage Three.

While Peterson and Rabe provide evidence of administrative cooperation in the implementation of federal programs, there is also evidence of continuing conflict between local and state bureaucrats. During the Congressional hearings on the Elementary and Secondary Education Consolidation Act of 1981, local school administrators voiced their fear of greater state control of local schools. Ironically, this legislation was designed to provide greater discretionary power to local and state governments in the management of federal programs.

For instance, one of the new professionals whom Peterson and Rabe considered to be part of the cooperative administrative structure, Dan Foster, administrative director, Projects, Compliance, and Research of the Hayward Unified School District, told the House subcommittee holding hearings on the 1981 legislation, "The LEA's [local education agency's] problem is not with federal interference in education, but rather with the state legislatures, state boards of education, and state departments of education."[32] At oversight hearings later in the year, Tom Rosica, executive director of the Office of Federal Programs in the Philadelphia school district, stated, "As I speak to my counterparts around the country, I think one of the concerns expressed is that we not replace federal bureaucracy with a state bureaucracy and federal regulations with state regulations."[33] At the same oversight hearings, Dan Foster again appeared, but this time as president of the Western Association of Administrators of State and Federal Programs, to express the fear on the part of local administrators of more control by state government.[34]

In summary, Peterson and Rabe appear to be correct about the development of cooperative relations between the new professionals responsible for federal programs at the state and local level. But it should also be recognized that these new professionals struggle with each other for control over the implementation of federal legislation. This results in political tension between the new professionals responsible for federal programs in local school districts and similar professionals in state education agencies. Therefore, the general evolution of the politics of implementation tends to be the following:

1. Federal legislation is implemented with minimum controls.
2. Interest groups and federal officials complain that state and local education agencies are not fulfilling the intent of federal legislation.
3. Federal regulations are tightened and made more specific.
4. New professionals appear in local and state education agencies to handle federal programs.
5. Complaints are voiced about federal red tape and regulation.
6. Federal controls are eased and cooperation develops between the new professionals in charge of federal programs.
7. Conflict continues between the new professionals at the state and local level.

THE POLITICS OF IMPLEMENTATION: POLITICIANS AND INTEREST GROUPS

In recent years, politicians have made the issue of federal red tape and control a major campaign issue. As part of its 1980s strategy to please conservative groups who were critical of federal involvement in education, the Republican party advocated limiting federal regulations over educational programs, and increasing local and state control. Such a policy would entail a major change in the way in which federal education laws are enforced. Of course, any change in the administration of federal programs brings an immediate response from interest groups. The methods of implementation of federal prorams are a product of actions by politicians, pressures from interest groups, and, as discussed in the last section, of conflict between bureaucrats.

In the 1980s, the Republican administration's plan for reducing federal regulations over educational programs and increasing local and state control was embodied in the Elementary and Secondary Education Consolidation Act of 1981. The general plan of the law was to lump large groups of categorical programs into block grants, and to have local and state educational agencies plan and administer the use of the money alloted for each grant.

The most controversial of the original proposals, which did not appear in the final legislation, was to combine money for the disadvantaged and the handicapped in the same block grant. Objections to this proposal were immediately raised by Representative Carl Perkins of Kentucky when introducing Secretary of Education Terrel Bell during the House hearings on the legislation. Perkins warned of potential conflict between interest groups representing the disadvantaged and the handicapped. He stated, "I am concerned about your bill because it could pit the disadvantaged and the handicapped against one another at the local level. It could also allow the use of these funds for local tax relief...."[35]

Secretary Bell's response to Representative Perkins and other critics of the proposal contained an interesting analysis of the political power of interest groups. Bell argued that the pressure of interest groups at the state level would ensure the proper allocation of federal funds. Bell told the committee, "The parents and those others who express themselves in lobbies when the legislature is in session, those forces would be at work, those handicapped children's advocates, the education associations and that big school lobby that is around every state house would be there."[36]

Referring to his own experience in state politics, Secretary Bell assured the committee that interest groups would determine the use of federal money. "I have lived in that arena," he claimed in reference to state politics. "We would presume that those forces would be protecting these interests. That state education lobby is a big one and it is powerful and the interest groups inside of education are getting more and more capable and powerful. We have the state school boards' association and the state teachers' associations. You know the scene. It is all that."[37]

From Secretary Bell's perspective, therefore, less federal regulation of educational programs would create more conflict between interest groups at the state level. On the other hand, interest groups objected to the withdrawal of federal control because they believed their interests would not be protected. M. Hayes Mizell, chairman of the National Advisory Council on the Education of Disadvantaged Children—an organization claiming to represent 6 million children who depend on Title I funds—complained to the House oversight committee, "The effect of the secretary's position is to create even more passive compliance with federal education law.... The federal bureaucracy has abandoned its responsibilities."[38]

Also objecting to the freedom provided under block grants were the new professionals described by Peterson and Rabe. Like some interest groups, the new professionals were also protected by stringent federal controls, and they objected to deregulation. They feared the potential battle with interest groups and legal problems. Members of the Florida, Georgia, North Carolina, Alabama, and California departments of education appeared before the House oversight committee and expressed fear about the lack of federal guidelines. Speaking for the state administrators, Steve Sauls of Florida stated, "Normally, we would be among the last to be complaining about the prospect of too little regulation. But we are concerned that too little regulation by the U.S. Department of Education will leave too many unanswered questions, with the result being that the courts will be asked to play a greater role in education policy making...."[39]

In summary, the implementation of federal legislation is part of the political battle between interest groups and bureaucrats. Conservative interest groups such as the Moral Majority and the Eagle Forum advocate a reduction in federal regulation and control. On the other hand, some interest groups such as those representing the disadvantaged and the handicapped feel protected by strong federal control. The new professionals at the state and local levels are concerned with any changes in regulations that threaten their interests. In addition, these new professionals compete for power over federal programs. It is within this complex arena of political struggle that federal regulations are developed and federal programs are administered.

CONCLUSION

Between the 1950s and the 1980s, federal involvement in education increased as grass roots movements sought federal aid to overcome injustices in educational opportunities; as politicians, after blaming the schools, called for educational reform to improve the economy and national defense; and as politicians discovered that organized groups interested in education could be a source of aid in campaigns and of votes.

Ironically, the reduction of federal involvement in 1980s symbolized the importance of education in national politics. In 1980, the

Republican party made educational issues an important part of its presidential campaign. In the future, the Democratic party, with its strong support from teachers' unions and other educational groups, could reverse this retreat. There is the possibility that federal involvement in education will change with each change of political control of the presidency and Congress. This will keep national education policy in a constant state of flux and confusion.

As national educational policy continues to change, the following guidelines can be used to analyze federal educational politics.

Method of Analysis

FEDERAL LEGISLATION

Determine the cause of the federal legislation:
1. Is the legislation a result of the failure of local and state education authorities to respond to a grass roots movement?
2. Is it the result of a politician or politicians seeking to form or to please a particular educational constituency?
3. Is it the result of politicians using education as a scapegoat for other national problems?
4. Is educational legislation being proposed as an easy cure for a complex national problem?

Determine the reasons for the content of the federal legislation:
1. What interest groups and politicians supported or opposed the legislation?
2. What political strategy was used to balance the desires of politicians and interest groups?
3. How was the above political strategy reflected in the content of the legislation?
4. Did an iron triangle develop between interest groups, federal administrators, and particular politicians?

APPOINTMENT OF FEDERAL EDUCATIONAL POLITICIANS

Determine the reasons for the appointment:
1. Was there pressure from a particular interest group?
2. Did the administration want to form a particular educational constituency?
3. Was the administration paying off a political debt?

Determine the consequences of the appointment:
1. What educational policies does the educational politician support?
2. How does the educational politician balance his or her educational

interests with pressures from interest groups, bureaucrats, and politicians?
3. What effect does the educational politician have on the implementation of legislation?

IMPLEMENTATION OF FEDERAL LEGISLATION

Determine the reasons for the methods of implementation:
1. Did the political party in power promise a particular method of implementation (e.g., deregulation and block grants under Republicans)?
2. What was the role of interest groups in developing the methods of implementation?
3. What role did local and state educational agencies play in developing the implementation methods?

Determine the consequences of the methods of implementation:
1. What government agency or agencies controls the federal program?
2. What interest group benefits?

NOTES

1. For instance, Richard K. Jung's recent review of research on the politics of education at the federal level, "The Federal Role in Elementary/Secondary Education: Mapping a Shifting Terrain," in Norman Boyan, ed., *Handbook of Research on Educational Administration* (White Plains: Longman, 1988) references only studies dealing with the implementation of policy.
2. Hugh Davis Graham, *The Uncertain Triumph: Federal Education Policy in the Kennedy and Johnson Years* (Chapel Hill: University of North Carolina Press, 1984), pp. 26–52.
3. Ibid., pp. 43–44.
4. Ibid., p. 48.
5. Ibid., pp. 71–72.
6. Ibid., pp. 73–75.
7. David Neal and David Kirp, "The Allure of Legalization Reconsidered: The Case of Special Education," in David Kirp and Donald Jensen, eds., *School Days, Rule Days: The Legalization and Regulation of Education* (Philadelphia: Falmer Press, 1986), pp. 346–48.
8. Ibid., pp. 349–50.
9. Graham, *Uncertain Triumph*, p. 190.
10. Diane Ravitch, *The Troubled Crusade: American Education 1945–1980* (New York: Basic Books, 1983), p. 308.
11. Phyllis Schlafly's letter was reprinted as "Please Excuse My Child from ..." in *School & Community*, Vol. 72, No. 1 (Fall 1985), 8.
12. Quoted in Bert Greene and Marvin Pasch, "Observing the Birth of the Hatch Amendment Regulations: Lessons for the Education Profession,"

Educational Leadership (December 1985/January 1986), p. 44.

13. Quoted by Senator Lowell Weicker in U.S. Senate, Committee on Labor and Human Resources, *Hearing on William J. Bennett, of North Carolina, to be Secretary of the Department of Education*, 97th Cong., 1st sess. (January 28, 1985), p. 61.

14. Ibid., pp. 173–74.

15. Ibid., pp. 60–61.

16. Ibid., p. 188.

17. Graham, *Uncertain Triumph*, p. 155.

18. Ibid., p. 156.

19. Ibid., p. 157.

20. National Commission on Excellence in Education, *A Nation at Risk: The Imperative for Educational Reform* (Washington, D.C.: U.S. Department of Education, 1983), pp. 5–7.

21. See Daniel Quinn Mills, "Decisions about Employment in the 1980s: Overview and Underpinning"; and Michael Wachter, "Economic Challenges Posed by Demographic Changes," in Eli Ginzburg et al., eds., *Work Decisions in the 1980s* (Boston: Auburn House, 1982).

22. Pamela Walters and Richard Robinson, "Educational Expansion and Economic Output in the United States, 1890–1969," *American Sociological Review*, Vol. 48 (August 1983), pp. 480–493.

23. U.S. Senate, Committee on Labor and Human Resources, Subcommmittee on Education, Arts, and Humanities, *Hearings on the Education for Economic Security Act*, 98th Cong., 1st sess. (March 8, 1982), p. 1.

24. Ibid., pp. 290–93.

25. Ibid., pp. 294–99.

26. Ibid., pp. 312–17.

27. Ibid., pp. 353–57.

28. Ibid., p. 365.

29. Paul Peterson and Barry Rabe, "The Evolution of a New Cooperative Federalism" in Norman Boyan, ed., *Handbook of Research on Educational Administration* (White Plains: Longman, 1988).

30. Ibid.

31. Ibid., p. 28.

32. U.S. House of Representatives, Subcommittee on Elementary, Secondary, and Vocational Education and Subcommittee on Select Education and Labor, *Joint Hearing on the Elementary and Secondary Education Consolidation Act of 1981*, 97th Cong., 1st sess. (May 28, 1981), pp. 113–14.

33. U.S. House of Representatives, Subcommittee on Elementary, Secondary, and Vocational Education, *Oversight Hearings on Title I, ESEA, and the Chapter 2 Education Block Grant.* 97th Cong. 1st sess. (October 6, 1981), pp. 21–22.

34. Ibid., pp. 23–27.

35. U.S. House of Representatives, *Joint Hearing on ESEA*, p. 44.

36. Ibid., p. 95.

37. Ibid., p. 95.

38. U.S. House of Representatives, *Oversight on Title I, ESEA*, pp. 30–31.

39. Ibid., pp. 44–45.

CHAPTER 4

State Politics of Education

The centralization of control of state educational policies is increasing the influence of business groups and teachers' associations. The trend toward centralization varies from state to state, depending on differences in political climate and government organization. Despite the fact that the U.S. Constitution, by not giving the power to control education to the federal government, gives it to state governments, state involvement in local schools has evolved slowly since the nineteenth century. In the nineteenth century, state governments were primarily concerned with laws creating school districts, general academic reqirements, and compulsory education. In the early twentieth century, most states began to license teachers and establish teacher certification standards. During these early years, state education agencies remained relatively small.

In the 1960s, state control over local schools increased with the administration of federal programs and the enforcement of civil rights policies. It was estimated that by 1983, 50 percent of the staff in state education agencies was supported by federal funds. In addition, court decisions in the 1970s requiring equitable financing of schools forced state governments to become more involved in local school finance and caused some state legislators to become experts in educational policy.

In the 1980s, state involvement in education increased with federal deregulation and block grants, and school reform. Block grants and deregulation increased the control of state education agencies over the planning and administration of federal programs. Governors and state legislators, taking their cues from national leaders, declared that improved schools would cure the states' economic problems. The resulting school improvement campaign increased state control over teacher certification and school curricula. Some states established statewide competency testing of teachers and students. In other states, legislatures actually restructured the teaching profession by establishing career ladders and master teacher plans. States like California, which have the power to influence textbook adoption in local school systems, pressured publishers to change the content of textbooks.

In summary, the historical trend is toward growing centralization of state power over education. In part, the continuation of this trend will depend on the shifting nature of educational politics at the national level, and the degree of resistance from local school systems. Of course, with greater centralization of power comes greater uniformity. Statewide testing and detailed curriculum requirements result in uniformity of content and curriculum in public schools and teacher training institutions. In addition, greater involvement in educational finance strengthens state control over local schools.

In this chapter, our discussion of state educational politics will begin with a description of the similarities and differences between states, and of the major political actors. We shall then discuss the causes for political action at the state level and present a method of analysis of state educational politics.

PATTERNS OF STATE EDUCATIONAL POLITICS

The increasing centralization of state educational policies and the influence of teachers' associations and business groups can be understood by analyzing differing patterns of state educational politics. Joseph McGivney provides the best synthesis of categories of state educational politics.[1] His theoretical framework assumes that as social organizations develop, they become more centralized and bureaucratized.

McGivney's categories are based on Lawrence Iannaccone's pioneering work, *Politics in Education*.[2] Iannaccone used four categories to describe state educational politics. In the first category, *Type I (Local-Disparate)*, political decisions are primarily the result of linkages between state politicians and local school board members and superintendents. In other words, power is located at the local level. In the second category, *Type II (Monolithic)*, state eductional politics are dominated by a coalition of statewide educational interest groups, including teachers' associations and associations of school administrators. In this category a coalition of educational interest groups applies pressure to members of the state legislature. In the third category, *Type III (Fragmented)*, political decisions are a product of conflict between educational interest groups, and between educational interest groups and state agencies. The cooperation of Type II politics is replaced with competition. Iannaccone modeled the last category, *Type IV (Syndical)*, on the Illinois School Problems Commission, which tried to establish a cooperative effort between government officials, education groups, and private citizens for the development of state educational policy.

Iannaccone assumes that state education systems evolve from the local-based character of Type I to the statewide syndical model of Type IV. In this evolutionary process, different states are at different levels of development. McGivney accepts the idea of stages of development but recasts Iannaccone's categories, using new research on state politics.

In McGivney's categories, state educational politics evolve to a centralized bureaucratic form. McGivney's Stage I is similar to Iannaccone's Type I, with educators primarily representing a local constitutency, and state education agencies and legislatures working to maintain local control. Like Iannaccone, McGivney labels Stage II "Monolithic" and describes a statewide coalition of educational interest groups working with key members of the legislature. In the context of development, the concerns of Stage II are broader than the local concerns of Stage I. In Stage III, the Monolithic structure is replaced with competition between educational interest groups, and new interest groups, such as parochial schools, become active.

For McGivney, Stage III is an important step in centralization because individual interest groups direct their attention to specific state agencies. In the Monolithic category, Stage II, interest groups primarily interacted with each other, and, as a group, with members of the state legislature. At Stage III, interaction between interest groups decreases as individual interest groups interact with specific state agencies. McGivney argues that Stage III is a product of increasing bureaucracy and centralization. At this stage, competition between interest groups results from a desire to protect their respective share of advantages won from government. In other words, as the role of state government in education increases, each educational interest group becomes dependent on a continuation of a particular state program or funds. At Stage II, interest groups begin to compete for more state support for their particular programs. This competition causes the coalition of Stage II to disintegrate.

McGivney replaces Iannaccone's Type IV or Stage IV with a model of a statewide bureaucracy in which iron triangles form between members of education lobbies, members of the state legislature, and representatives of the chief executive. In McGivney's words, "Over time ... increasing influence is gained by or is delegated to the bureaucracy as the former lobby becomes more and more the bureaucracy.... Conflict is accommodated through an impersonal, rational, and legalistic process that becomes dominated by the bureaucracy." [3]

McGivney matches his stages of development with Fredrick Wirt's national study of state centralization. After closely examining the laws, constitutions, and court decisions in each of the fifty states, Wirt constructs a School Centralization Scale to rate the degree of centralized state control as opposed to local control. While Wirt found varying degrees of centralization between states, the major gatekeeping functions of teacher certification, accreditation, and attendance were under rigid control even in the most decentralized state.

In general, Wirt concluded, state politics controls local school policies. Any reform movement that attempts change at the local level will have only a marginal impact. In Wirt's words, "If the locus of reform is the district or school site, efforts at reform, even if successful, win only a skirmish; the massive structure beyond it remains unengaged or unaffected." Therefore, Wirt argued, state politics of education is the key to understanding the organization and operation of local schools. "Too often, then," Wirt writes, "local politics is a marginal politics, a struggle over things at the fringe, with the major decisions about how children will be taught having already been made elsewhere and therefore almost untouchable locally." [4]

Accepting Wirt's argument about the power of state educational politics over local schools, McGivney matches Wirt's scale to his political stages. States rating low on the School Centralization Scale are in Stage I of state educational politics, and states rating high on Wirt's scale are in Stages II and III. Only one state, Hawaii, with complete state control of the schools, ranks at the top of Wirt's scale and is placed in McGivney's State IV. Examples of states in Stage I that rank low on the centralization scale are Connecticut, Massachusetts, Maine, and New Hampshire. Missouri, Texas, Rhode Island, Georgia, Illinois, and Tennessee are in Stage II; in Stage III are Wisconsin, New York, California, Colorado, New Mexico, Nebraska, Michigan, New Jersey, Minnesota, and Florida. [5]

The general patterns in state educational politics found by Iannaccone, Wirt, and McGivney create a picture of increasing centralization and control by state governments over local education. As educational control becomes more centralized and uniformity increases, the power of the individual citizen over local educational policy decreases and the range of educational choices becomes limited.

POLITICAL INFLUENCE

With centralization, the control of state educational policies is primarily a product of interaction between leading politicians and educational politicians, and between education associations and business groups. In Stage I of state politics, local school people and communities exert a major influence over state policies. By Stages III and IV, teachers' associations—usually the strongest of the eduational interest groups—and the business community compete for influence over politicians and educational politicians.

In addition, during the 1980s with the growing concentration of educational policy making at the state level, state governors made education a central focus of their political campaigns. As politicians, governors tried to please teachers' organizations and the business community. To the business community, governors promised an improved economic system through better schooling. To teachers, they promised improved salaries and a restructured profession. Sometimes governors were forced to choose one group over another. Most often the choice was the business community.

While there is a trend toward centralization and increased influence of statewide teachers' organizations and business groups, there are still differences in patterns of influence between different states. An important study of influence in state education politics was conducted by Catherine Marshall, Douglas Mitchell, and Fredrick Wirt. They synthesized previous studies of influence in state politics, and identified by order of influence the major political actors in Arizona, West Virginia, California, Wisconsin, Pennsylvania, and Illinois. Their study is useful for discussing general patterns of influence in state politics.[6]

One problem with the study is that it blurs distinctions between the influence of elected politicians and educational politicians, and that of groups acting outside the official sphere of government. Of course, this distinction is important at all levels of government. Obviously, elected politicians and educational politicians responsible for state eductional policy will exert a great deal of influence. The issue is which government actor has the most influence over education. Is the major influence in the government exerted by the governor, members of the state legislature, the state legislature as a whole, the chief state school officer, or the state education agency?

The next problem is identifying the group outside of government that exerts the most influence over politicians and educational politicians. For instance, if the governor is influential in educational policy making, then it is important to identify the group outside of government that influences the governor. Is the governor influenced by the power of the business community, teachers' associations, or other interest groups? The same question can be asked about members of the state legislature and state education agencies.

Unfortunately, Marshall, Mitchell, and Wirt do not distinguish between influences in government and influences on members of government. But even with this limitation, generalizations about influences on state education policies can be made from their study. For the six states in their study they established the following list, by order of influence, of policy actors at the the state level.

1. Members of the state legislature specializing in educational issues
2. The legislature as a whole
3. The chief state school officer and senior state officials in state departments of eduction
4. Coalitions of educational interest groups (teachers, administrators, school boards, and other education groups)
5. Teachers' associations
6. Governor and executive staff
7. Legislative staff
8. State boards of education
9. School board associations
10. Associations of school administrators
11. Courts
12. Federal policy mandates
13. Noneducation interest groups (business leaders, taxpayers' groups)
14. Lay groups (PTAs, school advisory groups)
15. Educational research organizations
16. Referenda
17. Producers of educational materials

This list can be divided between those inside and those outside of government. For instance, the following is a list, by order of influence, of those within government.

1. The state legislature
2. The chief state school officer and senior members of the state department of education
3. The governor and executive staff
4. Legislative staff
5. The state board of education

Focusing on influences within state governments, Marshall, Mitchell, and Wirt found that certain legislators specialized in educational issues and guided the votes of others. Most legislators gave educational issues only occasional attention. Obviously, the lawmaking power of a legislature would give it the greatest control over educational policy.

Next in order of influence, the power of chief state school officers varied significantly within the six states. In general, they functioned as long-term bureaucrats who worked patiently to establish educational policies. An earlier study of chief state school officers found them to be primarily white males in their middle 50s with rural backgrounds. Most chief state school officers come from the ranks of public school administrators and teachers. They exert their greatest influence within state departments of education and in their leadership of state boards of education. Elected chief state school officers, as opposed to appointed, tend to exert more influence among legislators.[7]

As Marshall, Mitchell, and Wirt note, governors increased their involvement in educational policy in the early 1980s. Prior to that time, governors were concerned mainly with school finance issues. A major study done in the 1970s concludes, "state tax burden, educational effort, and educational expenditures were associated most strongly with gubernatorial involvement in educational policy making."[8]

Members of legislative staffs gain their influence by acting as links between interest groups and members of the state legislature. Both legislators and interest groups depend on their expertise. The most influential staff members work for legislators who specialize in educational legislation.

And finally, at the bottom of the scale in influence are the state boards of education. In general, state boards of education are strongly influenced by the chief state school officer, who often sets the agenda for their meetings. State legislators and educational interest groups consider state boards of education as having only a minor role in policy making. In fact, very few board members believed they had any meaningful influence on legislative actions.[9]

Now the important issue is what groups outside of government have the greatest influence over policy makers in government. In the six states, government officials are influenced by the following list of groups in order of importance.

1. Education associations
2. Noneducation groups (business leaders, taxpayers' groups)
3. Lay groups (PTAs, school advisory groups)
4. Educational research organizations
5. Producers of educational materials

In the six states, eduction associations have the greatest influence on government officials. Teacher's associations are the most influential, with a coalition of educational associations running a close second. School board associations are slightly more influential than organizations representing school administrators. The combined figures for all six states give education groups more influence than noneducation groups—except Arizona, where the "Phoenix 40," a group of prestigious businesspeople that meets informally once a month, exercises strong influence over state educational policy.

In addition, the courts and federal policy mandates influence state educational policy. Court decisions have forced states to act in areas such as school finance, segregation, and education for the mentally retarded and handicapped. As discussed in the previous chapter, federal policy mandates have created a new group of professionals at the state level and established new educational programs. The courts and the federal government can, in some situations, exert more influence than any state government officials.

Important differences in influence exist between the six states. In West Virginia, the courts became active in 1979, when a ruling in *Pauley v. Kelley* mandated a very detailed reform of the state school system that included defining minimum standards and changing the system of educational funding. In Illinois, the chief state school officer and the state department of education have little influence, while teachers' associations are ranked very high.[10]

Different patterns of influence in each state cause variations in educational policies. In West Virginia, under the influence of the courts, equalizing access to education is a major concern. In Illinois, because of the strong influence of teachers' associations, collective bargaining is a major concern. In Wisconsin and Illinois, which have strong teachers' and local school board associations, there is a high level of interest in mandating local development of student tests. On the other hand, in West Virginia, California, and Pennsylvania, the influence of local school board associations is low and is related to a high interest in statewide student testing.

These variations highlight the ultimate impact of centralization. With centralization there are fewer groups and individuals influencing educational politics. Only the most powerful have meaningful influence, the most powerful being the teachers' associations and the business community.

In highly centralized states, the education associations protect their interests and support educational changes that will enhance their power and position. On the other hand, the business community supports educational policies that serve their economic interests, which usually means ensuring that the schools prepare students to meet their labor needs.

THE NATIONALIZATION OF STATE POLICIES

In recent years, several nongovernment organizations have been contributing to the nationalization of state educational policies. In this context, *nationalization* means creating uniformity in policies between states. Three of these organizations, the National Governors' Association, the Council of Chief State School Officers, and the Education Commission of the States, serve as forums for the discussion of educational policies and for the coordination of state educational efforts. The third type of nationalizing organization, private foundations, attempts to advance programs for educational change by influencing politicians at the state level.

In a larger sense, the efforts of these organizations represent a centralization of state educational policy beyond just centralization within a state. Consequently, influence over policies tends to be limited to the most powerful. One result is an emphasis on educational policies that serve economic interests.

In addition, these organizations tend to coordinate their efforts. In the 1980s such coordination was directly related to the increased involvement of governors in educational issues and the resulting strengthening of ties between governors through the Education Commission of the States. In an effort to strengthen their reform efforts, foundations also recruited educationally active governors to serve on task forces.

A good example of this interrelationship of activities is the report of the Task Force on Education for Economic Growth of the Education Commission of the States. The Education Commission of the States was founded in 1966 as a nonprofit, nationwide interstate compact to help state governments develop education policies. The organization strongly depends on outside funding from foundations and private corporations to support its coordinating activities. For instance, the Task Force on Economic Growth received support from fifteen leading corporations and foundations, including the Aetna Life & Casualty Insurance Foundation, AT&T, Control Data, Dow Chemical, Xerox, Time Inc., Texas Instruments, RCA, the Ford Motor Company Fund, and IBM.

The membership of the task force, which was almost evenly divided between state politicians and business leaders, exemplifies the coming together of state politicians and the business community in the formulation of eductional policy. The chair of the task force was Governor James Hunt of North Carolina, and the co-chairs were Frank Cary, chairman of the executive committee of IBM, and Governor Pierre S. du Pont of Delaware. In addition, there were eleven other governors and three members of state legislatures. Of the total of thirteen governors, four made the impact of educational reform on economic development a central focus of their political campaigns. These were the chair, Lamar Alexander of Tennessee, and the co-chair, Thomas Kean of New Jersey. The business community was represented by chief executive officers from fourteen of the most powerful coporations in the United States, including RCA, Texas Instruments, Ford Motor, Xerox, Dow Chemical, Control Data, and AT&T.

Interestingly, a comparison of financial supporters of the task force with its membership reveals that the corporations represented on the task force were also its major financial supporters. This created the interesting situation of corporations funding a task force that brought together state leaders and the business community for the purpose of formulating state educational policy.

This combination of forces produced a report, *Action for Excellence*, that primarily served the interests of the business community. The introduction declares, "We believe especially that businesses, in their role as employers, should be much more involved in the process of setting goals for education in America." Linking education to economic concerns, the report states, "If the business community gets more involved in both the design and the delivery of education, we are going to become more competitive as an economy." The report used the schools as a scapegoat for economic problems and singled out the reform of the teaching profession as the key to school and economic improvement.[11]

In addition to the Education Commission of the States, the National Governors' Association has tried to coordinate educational policies among the states. Until the 1980s, the organization paid little attention to broad eduational issues. But in 1985, the National Governors' Association established seven task forces to plan state educational improvement to the year 1991. The task force topics included teaching, leadership and management, parent involvement and choice, school readiness, technology, facilities, and college quality.[12]

A logical interest of governors is to enhance their prestige and power by concentrating control of education at the state level. This interest was reflected in a controversial proposal to allow states to declare school districts academically bankrupt. Taken as a last resort, the declaration would allow states to oust local officials and assume state control of a local school district. The major supporter of the idea, Governor Thomas Kean of New Jersey, stated, "As Governor of New Jersey, I couldn't sleep at night if I thought our schools were continuing to turn out unqualified graduates year after year after year, and I wasn't doing anything about it." [13]

In the 1980s, the Council of Chief State School Officers shared the same economic concerns as the governors. Many members of the organization, leading state educational politicians, were influenced by the same pressure groups as governors. For instance, in 1985, the organization studied the relationship between education and economic development. It decided to focus on the decreasing supply of high school graduates available for entry-level employment, the employment needs of small business, the impact of technology, and how education officials could attract new industry to their states. [14]

Of course, this agenda was dear to the hearts of the business community within each state. Of particular concern was at-risk youth. In the 1980s, the decreasing supply of high school graduates forced employers to dig deeper into the labor pool of poor and minority youth. After a decade of neglect, improving the education of the urban poor returned to the top of the policy agenda. In September of 1986, David W. Hornbeck, president-elect of the Chief State School Officers and Maryland superintendent of schools, told the council's study group that aiding at-risk youth was closely linked to state economic growth. He stressed that the way in which the schools dealt with this problem would affect the rate of economic growth within communities. [15]

Therefore, national organizations representing leading state politicians and educational politicians are primarily concerned with how a state's educational system can help solve its economic problems. While not conclusive evidence, this suggests that the business community is exerting the greatest influence on these nationalizing organizations. Interestingly, one focus of the effort to improve the economy by changing educational policy is on changing the profession of teaching through career ladders, master teacher programs, and certification requirements. If teachers' associations are rivals with the business community for influence in state politics, then one must question the motives of those attempting to change the profession. The basic political question that should be asked is whether or not the changes will increase or decrease the political influence of teachers. One might assume that the business community would want to decrease teacher power.

In fact, concern with reforming the teaching profession in the 1980s linked the National Governor's Association and another nationalizing influence, private foundations. The association recommended the establishment of a national board of teacher standards, an idea championed by the Carnegie Corporation of New York. In fact, the Carnegie Corporation's campaign for a national certification board and school reform provides a good example of how foundations can influence state policies. In its national campaign, the Carnegie Corporation tried to persuade states to change their teacher training and certification laws to conform to the recommendations of their task force report, *A Nation Prepared: Teachers for the 21st Century*. As part of this effort, the Carnegie Corporation granted $890,000 to the National Governors' Association for the purpose, in the words of Marc Tucker, executive director of the Carnegie Forum on Education and the Economy, of "helping states that want to empower teachers to do so." With this money, the National Governors' Association planned to aid states and local communities in implementing the foundation report.[16]

In addition, members of the Carnegie task force traveled to twenty-nine states between June and September of 1986 in an attempt to sell the ideas in the report, sold 35,000 copies of the report, and provided information and assistance to state legislative and gubernatorial aides. Marc Tucker defended the methods as not being just an advertising campaign. He stated, "We have not been marketing this report in the sense in which most people would use that term, developing advertising campaigns, trying to change people's opinions in an aggressive way. I don't think it's appropriate for us to do that." While denying being aggressive in their campaign, Tucker told an audience in Massachusetts, which included Governor Michael S. Dukakis, "The bottom line as I see it is that Carnegie has really fashioned a house of the future of teaching in the twenty-first century. They believe, and we believe, that Massachusetts is in a good position to take those proposals and run with them."[17]

If the Carnegie report were put into practice, then changes in state educational policy would include the recognition of a national certification board, changing state teacher education requirements, and the development of performance goals for schools. In fact, within three months of the issuance of the report, Carnegie staff members were claiming that they had directly influenced some state legislation. For instance, Carnegie staff members held small informal meetings with the governor of Washington State, Booth Gardner, who then proceeded to propose legislation based on the Carnegie report for graduate-level teacher education degrees and for giving more power to teachers at the school site. In Oregon, an education commission was organized with the aid of Vera Katz, a member of the Carnegie task force and Speaker of the House in Oregon. A commission member claimed that its recommendations would "parallel what was in the Carnegie report." When a two-and-a-half-day conference was organized in North Carolina by former Governor James Hunt, it was announced that an attempt would be made to see the state "put together a comprehensive package of ideas that would move some of the Carnegie proposals to reality." Similar claims of state activity occurred in Minnesota, California, and New Jersey.[18]

The combination of activities by foundations, the National Governor's Association, the Council of Chief State School Officers, and the Education Commission of the States increases the rate of centralization of state educational policies. This nationalization of state educational policies moves the pattern of state politics beyond McGivney's Stages III and IV. Consequently, it reduces the number of groups outside of government that influence educational policy, while increasing the importance of the governor.

The nationalizing trend in state educational politics adds a new stage to McGivney's patterns of state politics. McGivney stops at Stage IV-centralization, which, as discussed above, does not explain the full range of political patterns. A Stage V called "nationalization" should be added to complete the description of patterns of state educational politics. Table 4.1 provides a summary of patterns and influences in state educational politics.

SOURCES OF POLITICAL CHANGE

Like federal politics, there are three major sources of political change at the state level. These sources often overlap, and the following distinctions are therefore made for the purpose of analysis. One source of political change is grass roots movements. An example of a grass roots movement is the successful campaign in Minnesota for tuition tax credits. Another source is the political strategies of elected politicians and educational politicians. As an example, we shall discuss the activities of a master political strategist, Bill Honig, the superintendent of California schools. And third, the actions of Governor James B. Hunt of North Carolina will demonstrate how changes in educational issues are linked to broader policy concerns.

Grass Roots Movements

Tim Mazzoni and Betty Malen provide an excellent example of a grass roots movement in their research on tuition tax credit legislation in Minnesota between 1971 and 1981. They have analyzed the lobbying

TABLE 4.1 PATTERNS AND INFLUENCE IN STATE EDUCATIONAL POLITICS

Patterns of State Politics	
Stage I	Local-Disparate
Stage II	Monolithic
Stage III	Statewide-Disparate
Stage IV	Centralization
Stage V	Nationalization

Major Influences in State Educational Politics

Within State Government
1. State legislatures
2. Chief state school officers and senior members of state departments of education
3. Governors and executive staffs
4. Legislative staffs
5. State boards of education

Interest Groups
1. Education associations
2. Noneducation groups (business leaders, taxpayers' groups)
3. Lay groups (PTAs, school advisory groups)
4. Educational research organizations
5. Producers of educational materials

Government Agencies Outside of State Government
1. Courts
2. Federal policy mandates

Nationalizing Influences

1. National Governors' Association
2. Education Commission of the States
3. Council of Chief State School Officers
4. Foundations

techniques of the Minnesota Catholic Conference (MCC), representing six Catholic dioceses, and the Citizens for Educational Freedom (CEF), an organization composed of supporters of private schools.[19]

These two organizations formed an alliance in the late 1960s to campaign for state transportation aid for private schools. Following this campaign, the alliance sought state tax concessions for non-public-school pupils. As a single-issue lobbying group, the alliance constantly hounded state legislators regarding their attitudes toward financial aid to private schools. Their persistent efforts forced many legislators to bow to the pressure in order to avoid harassment or being labeled as opponents. According to Mazzoni and Malen, legislators placed the issue in the same category as gun control or abortion, where nonsupport of that single issue, no matter what other issues a politician stood for, would be considered sufficient reason by the voter to not support the politician.

In other words, a single-issue interest group will force a politician to support their position by making all other issues secondary. One unidentified member of the Minnesota legislature stated, "Their people [the MCC-CEF alliance] spoke out: 'We'll beat you if you vote against our bill.' And it didn't matter if you had done 5,000 things right.... That gave me and a lot of other people real concern ... and it was, I think, a statewide effort."[20]

The alliance campaigned with phone calls, orchestrated mailings, and persistent contact with state legislators. During the 1971 legislative debate on tuition tax credits, the alliance sent busloads of supporters to the state capitol to make direct contact with their representatives. Legislators reported that constituents would look them in the eye and say, "You aren't going to let us down now are you?"[21] Mazzoni and Malen quote legislators who pleaded for passage of the bill just to get alliance supporters off their backs. In addition, the alliance brought private-school supporters to legislative hearings to remind lawmakers of their promises. There were complaints that during the hearings on non-public-school aid, parents and kids flooded the hallways and legislative chambers.

The unanimous opinion of Minnesota legislators is that the successful passage of tax concessions for private schools in 1971, 1978, and 1981 was primarily due to the power of the MCC-CEF alliance. The key tactics of the alliance were identified as: "(1) keep the issue continuously on the legislative agenda; (2) energize sympathetic lawmakers to carry its bills, attract supporters to these bills, and maneuver them through the legislative process; and, most important, (3) mobilize grassroots constituency pressure to sway votes in the Legislature." And, from the standpoint of Mazzoni and Malen, the constant face-to-face contacts between lobbyists and lawmakers was the most effective lobbying technique.[22]

Another contributing factor to the success of the alliance was the lack of a well-organized opposition. Traditionally, the two teachers' unions have led strong national opposition to any form of tax concession to private schools. But, according to Mazzoni and Malen, the Minnesota Education Association and the Minnesota Federation of Teachers did not concentrate any effort on the issue raised by the

MCC-CEF alliance. Unlike the alliance, the two unions did not try to impose a political price on legislators who supported tax concession legislation. With no strong opposition from such a major influence in state educational politics, the alliance was able to achieve an easy victory.

Political Strategies

As briefly mentioned in Chapter 1, Bill Honig, California state superintendent of schools, is a master of political strategy. He set out, after his election in 1982, to build a state coalition that would support his proposed educational reforms. Honig decided that he needed the support of the education community. California teachers' unions and school administrators gave a great deal of time and money to the campaign of his opponent. In fact, after the 1982 election teachers wore black armbands to school. Honig decided to combine proposals for increased academic requirements, more homework, and the firing of incompetent teachers with support for a $950 million increase in state education funding. This, as he states, was his carrot to the education community.

First, he made the proposal for increased funding to the State School Boards Association and leading school administrators. Then he turned his attention to the local school superintendents, who were complaining that their communities did not support increased academic requirements for math, science, and English. To these local educational politicians, he held out the promise of more state money for their support of his reforms.

Money was also his method for wooing the teachers' unions. He recognized that their support was crucial for any reform movement. Honig writes, "Education reform without their support [the teachers] would be like Normandy Beach without the landing craft—a nonevent. It is they who command the classroom."[23] To outstanding California teachers he promised an extra $4,000 a year. In addition, he established regular meetings with leaders of the California Teachers' Association and the California Federation of Teachers to discuss the future training of teachers and to prevent misunderstandings regarding his reform program. But even with these efforts, Honig admitted, teachers were reluctant to give full support to his reform package.[24]

Honig recognized that the two most influential groups in state educational politics were the teachers' associations and the business community. To win support of the business community, he spoke at local meetings of the Kiwanis Club, Rotary Club, and chambers of commerce. And, on encountering a clipping in the *Los Angeles Times* listing the heads of California's top 100 corporations, Honig phoned each corporate head with a request that they write a letter to the governor supporting additional state funding for the public schools.[25]

His appearances before local business clubs were supplemented with community rallies organized by a nonprofit organization called the Quality Education Project. This organization's manual gives procedures for organizing local education rallies designed to attract 1,000 to 10,000 people. The QEP provides videotapes to local groups on how to use the school auditorium or stadium and how to function as rally leaders. Certainly a very innovative method of gaining political support, the rallies are held with balloons and flags, emotional speechs and songs; and against this background, parents are asked to sign pledges to support the schools. The emotional quality of these rallies was captured by comments made by a World War II veteran in San Luis Obispo, California, to a newspaper reporter. The veteran told the reporter, "I haven't had feelings like this since I was in uniform. I realized something for the first time tonight. It's just not American to be against the public schools."[26]

Building support from minority groups was another important part of Honig's strategy. He went directly to the black and Hispanic communities in California with speeches promising quality education. "The response," Honig writes, "was enthusiastic; the audiences themselves suggested that the main victims in the decline of the public-school standards had been their children."[27]

Careful organization of business leadership, minority leadership, community rallies, and school leadership (without the support of the teachers' association) was the key to Honig's eventual victory. But, Honig admits, not all of it was sheer political brillance on his part. For instance, when he was fighting the governor to gain the carrot of his plan, increased state funding, luck became a major factor. According to Honig, in the middle of the debate on the state budget, President Reagan visited a predominantly Hispanic high school in Los Angeles that was noted for its academic success. Surrounded by reporters, President Reagan stopped to chat with a student who had complained that possible cutbacks in state funds would reduce the school's programs. After the article was published in the *Los Angeles Times*, Honig said he received a call from the governor's office with a promise to increase the state school budget.[28]

Honig's methods embody all the important elements in state educational politics. Linkages were established with important power groups, including business and school leaders. Honig admits that his major failure was not winning the support of the teachers' associations. The support he received from the minority community is an important element in states with large minority populations. In addition, Honig made direct linkages to local communities through his public-school rallies.

General Policy Concerns

In the early 1980s, many governors tried to capitalize on apparent public dissatisfaction with the public-school system. Most often, they would link claims of school failure with economic problems. This action paralleled the political use of education by national leaders. First, governors would use schools as scapegoats for general problems facing their states. During the early 1980s, this meant blaming the schools for problems in their states' economies. Second, they claimed that school reform would solve their states' problems.

Governor James B. Hunt of North Carolina typifies this pattern. He claimed, "Our economic future is in danger because our students, unlike those in other leading industrial nations, are not learning the fundamental skills they need in a modern economy." [29] Blaming the U.S.'s low rate of increase in productivity in comparison to those of Japan and West Germany on the public schools, Governor Hunt argued that one cause lay in the differences in academic requirements and the quality of teachers.

Reflecting his participation on the Task Force on Education for Economic Growth of the Education Commission of the States, Governor Hunt advocated the establishment of state task forces that would include leaders of business, education, and labor. Each task force, he argues, should develop a plan that matches educational objectives with economic objectives. In addition, each plan should include a timetable and a method for evaluating results. Alongside the work of the state task forces, would be partnerships between education, business, and government. Governor Hunt was quite clear in his determination to have business play the dominant role in these partnerships. He wrote, "A central element of our plan is the involvement of business as a genuine partner with the schools, to help determine what is taught, to assist in marshaling the resources needed to provide top-quality education, and to convey to educators the skills that are needed in the workplace." [30]

In his own state, Governor Hunt created the North Carolina Commission on Education for Economic Growth. While Governor Hunt, in his role on the Task Force on Education for Economic Growth, called for the involvement of organized labor, he included no representatives of labor on his state's commission. The fifty-member group consisted of legislators, top business and corporate leaders, educators, school board members, and students. In other words, the planning for education for economic growth involved an alliance of government, business, and education.

In addition to the Commission on Education for Economic Growth, Governor Hunt created the North Carolina Business Committee on Math/Science, with the specific goal of expanding the involvement of local business in math and science programs in the public schools. Governor Hunt proudly boasted, "We have involved North Carolina businesses and industries in the schools to an unprecedented degree." [31]

Against this background of linking educational policies to economic problems, North Carolina instituted in the early 1980s a variety of reforms. Minimum competency tests in reading, writing, and mathematics were required of public-school students. A tuition-free residential high school for mathematics and science was established. Students were honored through the North Carolina Scholars Program. Money was provided for additional summer training of high school math and science teachers, and the Quality Assurance Program was instituted to monitor teacher education programs.

In summary, state politicians, in a manner similar to national politicians, link schools to general policy issues. First, they blame the schools and then they declare that they are the cure. What with the growing centralization of state control and the decreasing number of influential groups outside of government, the business community has begun to wield a major influence over state educational policies. Of course, this pattern can be modified through the pressure of organized interest groups like the previously discussed the MCC-CEF alliance in Minnesota.

CONCLUSION

The following series of questions provides a method for analyzing state educational politics. The questions are divided into three categories dealing with political patterns, and influence inside and outside government.

Method of Analysis of State Educational Politics

POLITICAL STYLE
1. Are the most important political contacts in educational policy making betweeen government officials and local school authorities?

2. Do the major state educational groups work together to influence policy making in state government?
3. Are iron triangles established between particular educational interest groups and state agencies?
4. Do educational interest groups compete with each other for influence over state educational policies?
5. Is there centralized control of state educational policy making?

EDUCATIONAL POLICY MAKING IN GOVERNMENT
1. Who are the key legislators interested in educational issues?
2. Has the governor made educational issues a primary focus of his or her campaign?
3. Does the chief state school officer have a strong influence in the state legislature?
4. Does the chief state school officer have a major influence on public opinion regarding educational policies?
5. Is the state board of education highly visible to the public and influential in the state legislature?

INTEREST GROUPS
1. Which educational interest group has the most influence in state government?
2. What organizations represent business interests at the state level?
3. In the consideration of educational issues, does the governor or other major state government leaders favor one interest group over another?
4. Is there a single-issue interest group operating in the state? Does the interest group exact a political cost for nonsupport of their issue?

NOTES

1. Joseph H. McGivney, "State Educational Governance Patterns," *Educational Administration Quarterly*, Vol. 20, No. 2 (Spring 1984), 43–63.
2. L. Iannaccone, *Politics in Education* (New York: Center for Applied Research in Education, 1967).
3. McGivney, "State Educational Governance," p. 54.
4. Frederick Wirt, "School Policy Culture and State Decentralization," in Jay D. Scribner, ed., *The Politics of Education* (Chicago: University of Chicago Press, 1977) pp. 186–187.
5. McGivney, "State Educational Governance," pp. 56–57.
6. Catherine Marshall, Douglas Mitchell, and Frederick Wirt, "The Context of State Level Policy Formation," Paper given at the American Educational Research meeting in San Francisco, California, April 16–20, 1986.

7. R. Campbell and T. Mazzoni, *State Policy Making for the Public Schools* (San Francisco: McCutchan, 1976), pp. 81–134.

8. Ibid., p. 172.

9. Ibid., pp. 46–47.

10. Marshall, Mitchell and Wirt, "State Level Policy Formation," pp. 13–29.

11. Task Force on Education for Economic Growth, *Action for Excellence* (Denver: Education Commission of the States, 1983), p. 18.

12. Chris Pipho, "Governors Push Better Schools Coalition," *Phi Delta Kappan*, Vol. 68, No. 2 (October 1986), 101–2.

13. Bill Montague, "State Takeovers Debated as School-Reform Tactic," *Education Week*, Vol. 6, No. 3 (September 24, 1986), 1, 17, 18.

14. Bill Montague, "Citing Link to Economy, School Chiefs Plan Study of 'At Risk' Students' Needs," *Education Week*, Vol. 6, No. 4 (October 1, 1986), 1, 13.

15. Ibid., p. 13.

16. Lynn Olsen, "Carnegie Backs Reform Agenda with Money, Effort," *Education Week*, Vol. 6, No. 6 (October 15, 1986), 1, 16.

17. Ibid., p. 16.

18. Ibid., p. 16.

19. Tim Mazzoni and Betty Malen, "Mobilizing Constituency Pressure to Influence State Education Policy Making," *Educational Administration Quarterly*, Vol. 21, No. 2 (Spring 1985), 91–116.

20. Ibid., p. 102.

21. Ibid., p. 103.

22. Ibid., p. 104.

23. Bill Honig, *Last Chance for Our Children* (Reading, Mass.: Addison-Wesley, 1985), p. 147.

24. Ibid., pp. 149–63.

25. Ibidl., pp. 118–19.

26. Ibid., p. 198.

27. Ibid., pp. 113–14.

28. Ibid., p. 119.

29. James B. Hunt, "Education for Economic Growth: A Critical Investment," *Phi Delta Kappan*, Vol. 65, No. 8 (April 1984), 538.

30. Ibid., p. 539.

31. Ibid., p. 541.

CHAPTER 5

Local Politics of Education

The nature of the local economy, the characteristics of the population, and the existence of community factions influence the style of local politics of education. In addition, local schools operate in the context of laws, programs, and regulations from state and federal governments. Each swing in federal policies causes local systems to change or initiate new programs. In the 1970s, in response to federal and state initiatives, local school systems instituted career education programs and expanded vocational education. This trend changed in the 1980s as concerns with America's declining position in world trade and desires to improve the economies of individual states created a demand for higher academic requirements.

While local school systems are often pawns in the strategies of state and federal politicians, each school district adapts education policies to the characteristics of its population. For instance, upper-middle-class suburbs tend to emphasize the education of students for jobs requiring a college education. In contrast, graduates of some rural and suburban school districts enter agricultural and factory occupations requiring little formal education. In these communities, the emphasis is on a solid general or vocational education with college preparatory courses being offered to a select few.

Urban schools must educate for a diversified labor market and deal with large numbers of poor and minority students. Consequently, urban schools offer a wide variety of educational programs ranging from advanced academic programs to highly specialized vocational training. The diversification of urban school programs has been aided by the development of magnet, or alternative, schools.

Magnet, or *alternative, schools* developed under pressure from the federal government to provide equality of educational opportunity. As discussed in Chapter 3, because of the lack of response from local school systems, civil rights groups were forced to turn to the federal government for aid. Magnet schools were a conservative response to demands for school desegregation. Rather than relying on forced busing to achieve integration, magnet schools promised voluntary compliance by offering specialized education programs that would attract students from differing racial backgrounds. Early alternative schools offered programs in the creative and performing arts, specialized academic training, and an emphasis on particular methods such as Montessori. As magnet school programs expanded in the 1980s, they became more directly linked to the needs of local labor markets. For instance, Houston established a high school to serve the petrochemical industry, and Atlanta created a school to supply workers to its financial district.[1]

Of course, every local school district must deal with problems that are peculiar to its setting and population. Sometimes these local issues overwhelm concerns with educating for the needs of local labor markets. The most divisive issues center on religious values and censorship. In some school districts, Protestants and Catholics war over support of public schools and the moral content of instruction. In these communities, health and sex education and increases in school taxes can be major areas of dispute. Reflecting attitudes in the national Republican party, Protestant fundamentalists in some school districts have battled against secular humanism and demanded censorship of school texts.

Value conflicts pose a major problem for public schools in a democratic and highly diverse society. No matter what values are reflected in the curriculum, they are bound to offend some group. And when the schools try to avoid any teaching of particular religious values, then, as is the case with Protestant fundamentalists, they are charged with being "godless."

Therefore, local educational politics will vary according to the needs of the local economy and the existence of factional disputes. Let us consider four models for analyzing local educational politics. These four models include most aspects of local school politics; they do not, however, consider the power of local teachers' unions and of local school bureaucracies. These aspects of local power will be discussed later in the chapter. Also, like most analytical models, they leave a great deal of room for variation; for instance, some communities might show the characteristics of several different models.

PATTERNS IN LOCAL POLITICS OF EDUCATION

We shall assume that there is a relationship between a community's labor needs and the community power structure that controls the schools. In some situations, labor market needs are secondary to strong factional disputes. We also assume that the nature of the power structure determines the type of school board and superintendent. As will be discussed in a later section, this may not be the case with local educational bureaucracies and teachers' unions.

The analytical models developed in this section are based on the work of Donald McCarty and Charles Ramsey.[2] They provide classifications of community power structures, school boards, and administrative styles. In creating these classifications, they have assumed that the community power structure determines the nature of the school board and the superintendent's administrative style. The following are the types of community power structures:

1. dominated
2. factional
3. pluralistic
4. inert

In a *dominated community*, majority power is exercised by a few persons or one person. In most cases, these people are part of the community's economic elite, though in some cases they are leaders of ethnic, religious, or political groups. Dominated power structures exist primarily in small towns and urban areas where the school system serves the needs of a labor market that is either diversified or dominated by a single industry. A major characteristic of a dominated power structure is the lack of a strong opposition.

Factional communities, as described by McCarty and Ramsey, usually have two factions that compete for influence. Very often these factions hold different values, particularly religious values. Each faction often shares equal power over school affairs. In these communities, concerns with the needs of the labor market are often secondary to religious issues.

In *pluralistic power structures*, there is competition between several community interest groups, with no single group dominating school policies. Often, a pluralistic power structure indicates a high degree of community interest in the schools, with many groups active in school affairs. McCarty and Ramsey found pluralistic power structures to be characteristic of suburban school systems where there is a high interest in students gaining access to occupations that require a college education.

Inert communities are without any visible power structure. McCarty and Ramsey claim that this situation most often occurs in rural communities in which the power is latent in the status quo of the community. If the status quo is disrupted, a power structure will appear. In the case of inert communities, there is little or no competition for positions on the school board. Membership usually goes to anyone who is willing to take on the job, and there is little public interest, as compared to other communities, in the schools. In these communities, most students do not intend to enter occupations for which education is a major factor. The primary concern is with a solid general or vocational education for most students and a college preparatory curriculum for a select few.

McCarty and Ramsey relate community power structures to types of school boards. The following depicts these relationships:

Community Power Structures	*Types of School Boards*
1. dominated	1. dominated
2. factional	2. factional
3. pluralistic	3. status congruent
4. inert	4. sanctioning

A *dominated school board* shares the beliefs and values of the community elite. Often, economic control is a factor in an elite's influence on board members. The community elite can be represented by a majority on the board or several powerful individuals. Usually, there is no organized opposition for positions on the school board.

In *factional communities*, elections to the school board are often hotly contested, with board members representing the beliefs and values of particular factions. Power between factions can shift with the election of new members. Members of a *status-congruent school board* are not bound to a particular ideological position. In a *pluralistic power structure*, board members represent a wide variety of community groups. Board meetings emphasize discussion and consensus, with little influence from any particular community group.

Sanctioning school boards exist in communities with Inert power structures. This type of board is relatively inactive, and its members do not represent factions within the community. The term "sanctioning" refers to the tendency of this type of board to primarily follow its leadership and approve the recommendations of the school administrative staff.

McCarty and Ramsey argue that school boards hire compatible superintendents. In other words, there is a direct relationship between the community power structure, the nature of the school board, and the style of the superintendent. And, as we shall see, these relationships are all connected to the occupational aspirations of the local community.

Let us now consider these interrelationships in dominated, factional, pluralistic, and inert communities. Again, the reader is cautioned that the models developed in each section are for the purpose of analysis and that some communities might exhibit traits of several models.

Dominated Communities

In a community where the school board is dominated by an elite power structure, the superintendent will reflect the values of the power structure and act in their interests. Usually, this type of superintendent carries out board policies but does not initiate new policies.

For example, in a dominated community studied by McCarty and Ramsey, the elite power structure acted behind the scenes, with direct control of the school system being exercised by a superintendent who reflected their values.[3] In this town of 35,000, the school board was composed of seven members who were not high in the power structure and who were not troublemakers. The superintendent gave the appearance of being a strong decision maker with a firm hold on his job. The event that activated the community's elite power structure was the decision by four members to fire the superintendent because they felt he was overly involved in educational research and publication and was neglecting the school system. The superintendent was incredulous when first informed of the decision and did little to find other employment or prepare to leave the position. At a later board meeting, members asked if he had sought other employment, and when informed that he hadn't, they voted four to three to fire him. Immediately, the superintendent called the vice president of one of the two largest banks and the general manager of the largest company in the community. They were surprised by the firing, and the company manager got in contact with the presidents of two other banks, the local newspaper editor, and a lawyer from a highly prestigious family in town.

First, this group of community leaders met in the office of the vice president of the bank and decided to meet as a group with the superintendent before making a decision. At the next meeting, also held at the bank, the superintendent demanded a new contract and an increase in salary. After lengthy discussion, the town leaders decided to avoid community conflict and let the superintendent be fired.

The power of this elite group was evidenced in the plans that followed their decision. First, the group felt that the school board had gotten out of control. The most respected member of the elite group was made chairman of the school board's nomination committee, and its members were selected to assure elite control. This committee recommended candidates for the school board who were either members of the power structure or loyal followers. Traditionally, those recommended by the nomination committee had been elected without opposition to the school board. And finally, the leading members of the community kept a close watch on the nominating committee for several years to ensure the selection of the right candidates. In addition, a new superintendent was selected who, it was believed, would act in the interests of the town leaders.

McCarty and Ramsey argue that in this situation the superintendent made several mistakes. His major error was not recognizing that he was a servant of the power structure. He should have immediately gone to the elite group about the possible firing. Instead, the superintendent tried to play political strategist by bringing the elite group together and demanding a new contract and increased pay. These demands alienated the elite and created the possibility of open conflict.

From McCarty's and Ramsey's analysis of dominated communities, there emerges a pattern of educational policies resulting from elite control. First, elite leaders, particularly business leaders, want low taxes. Second, the leaders want the school to provide a curriculum that meets their needs. In most situations, this means a college preparatory curriculum for their children and a curriculum to prepare future employees. Finally, elite leaders want to reduce community conflict. This was precisely how the new superintendent acted in the dominated community studied by the two researchers.

In *Politicial Strategies in Northern School Desegregation*, David Kirby, T. Harris, and Robert Crain highlight the important role of elite groups in urban school politics. They studied ninety-one cities ranging in size from 50,000 to over 250,000. Their major conclusion is that urban elites have been the most important political actors in determining school desegregation plans. In their words, "school desegregation is a political decision made by the elites rather than the masses."[4]

Kirby, Harris, and Crain identified urban elite decision makers as being primarily drawn from the business community. In their study, over 50 percent of the elite were bankers, industrialists, and heads of local businesses. Only 5 percent of this decison-making group was composed of liberals who represented labor and civil rights organizations. The remainder of the elite decision makers were heads of local utilities, newspaper people, members of civic associations, executives, clergy, university administrators, and professionals.

Elite domination does not result in a uniform political style in all urban areas. Kirby, Harris, and Crain found that large, slow-growing cities with identifiable ethnic populations have liberal elites. They defined a liberal as someone who is willing to change the social structure to solve social and economic problems. On the other hand, they define a conservative as someone who wants to maintain existing social arrangements and expect individuals to adapt to those arrangements. They found conservative elites in smaller, faster-growing cities with relatively small ethnic populations.

Elite domination in urban areas is aided by school board elections that are nonpartisan and at-large. Of course, in some cities such as Chicago, the board of education is appointed by the mayor. In these situations, board appointments are determined by the political obligations of the mayor. Very often these political obligations are linked to the power of local elites. For instance, in Chicago in the early 1980s, the mayor appointed the entire slate recommended by the local business group, Chicago United.[5]

Nonpartisan and at-large elections were instituted in the early part of the twentieth century in order to clean up corrupt big-city school systems by ending the power of political parties. In effect, these changes ensured the domination of school board elections by business groups. An at-large election, as opposed to an election from a small district in a city, requires that a candidate campaign throughout the entire urban area. Campaigning within a small district in an urban area requires only a minimum of expense and organization. In many situations, the candidate can campaign simply by going door-to-door. Therefore, at-large elections require more money and organization. Since nonpartisan elections remove the influence of political parties, the candidate must turn to other sources of financial and organizational support. In most cases, these other sources are community business groups.[6]

Studies of nonpartisan urban elections have revealed a bias in favor of business and conservative groups. In *Nonpartisan Elections and the Case for Party Politics*, Willis Hawley argues that nonpartisan elections create a partisan bias in favor of Republicans.[7] These Republican politicians receive the majority of their support from the business community. Hawley studied nonpartisan elections in eighty-eight cities and concluded that they definitely favored the Republican business community. This was particularly true in cities with populations over 50,000 and that had many unemployed persons with low incomes and levels of education.

Hawley believes that the Republican bias in nonpartisan elections is caused by the relationships established through informal business ties and civic organizations. Without the active involvement of political parties, these informal networks assume a dominant role. Hawley emphasizes that there is a positive association between high socioeconomic class and participation in community organizations. It is almost impossible for a poor person to become part of an informal business network or join the local chamber of commerce.

It is these informal business networks, as McCarty and Ramsey also found, that control nominations to the school board in dominated communities. Sometimes an actual nominating committee will be created by community leaders. In dominated communities this nominating committee often controls school board elections. In other situations, actual business organizations will recommend candidates.

In the 1980s, the linkages between business groups and urban school systems were formalized by attempts to make education serve the needs of local labor markets. One pioneer agreement was the *Boston Compact* that was signed between the Boston public school system, the Tri-Lateral Council, and the Private Industry Council in Boston. The Tri-Lateral Council originated in 1974 and grew out of elite concerns with the desegregation of Boston schools. It is composed of representatives from the Greater Boston Chamber of Commerce, the National Alliance of Businessmen, and the Boston School Department.

The Boston Compact specifically links the goals of Boston schools to the needs of the local labor market. The compact states, "as the largest school system in Massachusetts, the Boston public schools must improve to sustain economic growth in the city." The school system agrees to improve the employability of its graduates, and the business community agrees to give hiring priority to job applicants residing in Boston.[8]

In Atlanta a similar arrangement exists between the schools and the business community. The Atlanta Partnership of Business & Education was chartered by the state of Georgia in order "to enhance the economic development potential of Atlanta and to improve the standard of living of its people by raising the educational achievement of its citizenry." To meet this goal, magnet schools in Atlanta are organized so that each program is answerable to business needs. Each magnet school has an advisory committee that is formed from the membership of the Atlanta Partnership. This committee, according to the report of the Atlanta Partnership, "provides continual counsel so that the curriculum and its delivery stay attuned to the developments within the industry."[9]

In other parts of the nation, formal ties between business and the schools were increased through *adopt-a-school programs*, with local businesses and industries adopting individual schools. This national movement is designed to increase the influence of business interests over public school curricula. As mentioned in Chapter 4, governors across the nation backed the implementation of adopt-a-school programs.

Compacts between schools and businesses, partnerships, and adopt-a-school programs are visible signs of the informal control traditionally exerted by local business groups. In dominated communities, business groups maintain their influence through their informal control of school boards. The primary goal, of course, is to ensure that the schools serve the needs of the local labor market.

Based on the study by McCarty and Ramsey, Figure 5.1 describes the development of educational policies in dominated communities. A local elite group indirectly controls the school board by controlling the nomination of its members. In turn, this dominated board selects a functionary superintendent who supports policies favored by the elite. These policies tend to be low taxes, a curriculum that meets the needs of the local labor market, a curriculum for the children of the elite, and a school system that operates with mimimum conflict.

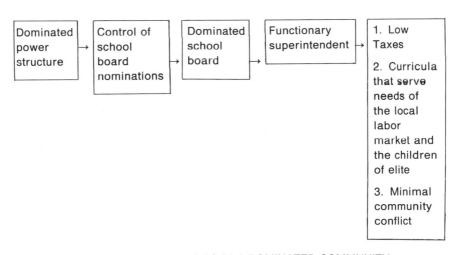

FIGURE 5.1 EDUCATIONAL POLICIES IN A DOMINATED COMMUNITY

Factional Communities

In contrast to the appearance of calm shown by dominated school boards, factional boards display a great deal of conflict. Unlike the functional superintendent, the superintendent in the factional community must be a political strategist who can balance competing groups.

In a factional community studied by McCarty and Ramsey, the major competition occurred between a permissive Jewish group and a conservative Catholic group.[10] With almost equal populations in the school district, the control of the school board shifted between groups in each highly contested election. The campaigns were very emotional, with each group accusing the other of undermining the quality of education.

When McCarty and Ramsey arrived in the community, the liberals on the school board had lost their majority to conservatives, who immediately fired the superintendent. The fired superintendent, according to McCarty and Ramsey, failed as a political strategist because he appeared to favor the previous liberal majority. Interviews with community members revealed that they clearly recognized the existence of the two factions, with each side admitting to secret meetings to plan strategy against its opponents.

The researchers found that factionalism in this community did not always mean a split vote. Many educational issues do not relate to factional divisions, and in some cases there is an attempt to avoid factional voting. But some situations do result in factional votes. For instance, in this particular community elementary school report cards became a heated issue. Liberals favored a card that simply reported "satisfactory," "unsatisfactory," and "excellent," based on a child's potential lerning rate. Conservatives wanted a card that gave grades of A through F, based on percentage test scores. The conservative majority rewrote the report card in one and half hours, with four conservative board members voting for the new card and three liberals voting against it.

In other communities, the most frequent types of factions are:

1. religious groups
2. racial groups
3. ethnic groups
4. taxpayers' groups
5. town people versus gown people (college communities)

Religious divisions are one of the most frequent causes of community factionalism. In most cases, this involves Catholics struggling against Protestants or Jews. Since most Catholics send their children to parochial schools, they are primarily interested in keeping down the costs of local public schools and ensuring that the teachings of the public schools are not in conflict with Catholic doctrines. For instance, a major debate in communities with large Catholic populations usually takes place over teachings about birth control and abortion in sex education courses.

Racial factions often develop over concerns with minority students gaining equal access to the labor market. Since the civil rights struggles of the 1950s, minority groups have campaigned to place their representatives on boards of education. Once on the board, minority group representatives back decisions directly related to the interests of their constituencies. In recent years, this has meant support for quality integrated education and additional programs for the disadvantaged. A major goal is to provide equal educational opportunities to ensure that minority students gain equality of opportunity in the labor market. In certain areas, ethnicity is an important factor. A Jewish, Italian, Irish, or Scandinavian name on the ballot might be attractive to ethnic-oriented voters.[11]

Sometimes communities will divide over school taxes. Many taxpayers' associations oppose increased spending by any part of the local government. McCarty and Ramsey state that the true leadership of taxpayers' associations is often unknown; such groups count on the support of the "silent majority" in a community to defeat attempts to increase school taxes and expenses.[12]

Town-and-gown conflicts often plague college towns, with faculty members wanting a more liberal and academic schooling than do town people. Town people usually disdain the ivory tower demeanor of professors, and professors often regard town people as culturally backward. This division can result in factional conflict over the curriculum, school activities, and grading policies.

The issue of *secular humanism* has divided many communities in the 1970s and 1980s. A classic dispute occurred in 1974 over textbook adoptions in Kanawha County, West Virginia. In varying degrees, the extreme emotional outbursts in this situation were later repreated in other communities.

An insightful analysis of the Kanawha County controversy is provided by Ann Page and Donald Clelland. They identify the source of the controversy as the attempt to protect a fundamentalist life-style against the pressures of modernity. In contrast to school battles that center on economic issues, life-style politics involves conflicts over beliefs and ways of living. In the words of Page and Clelland, "Life-style concern is most clearly evident when fading majorities come to recognize the eclipse of their way of life through loss of such control [over socialization in the schools]."[13]

In Kanawha County, the life-style issue erupted in June of 1974, when a school board member demanded greater board control of textbook selection and, after speaking at a local Baptist church, organized a demonstration by 1,000 antitextbook protesters at a school board meeting. By September, protesting parents picketed local businesses and mines in the county and withheld approximately 10,000 children from the school system.

Violence quickly escalated with the firebombing of two schools, the shooting of a picketing protester, the destroying of school property, and the dynamiting of the county education building. In the midst of this violence, a citizens' review board split into two factions, with the antitextbook group being in the minority. The majority faction recommended that all but 35 of the 325 books under protest be returned to the classroom, and the minority faction recommended that 180 books be permanently banned. Of course, the majority faction had its way, and most of the books were returned to the classroom, with 35 of the most controversial books being placed in the school library. The protesters reacted to this decision by having four board members and the superintendent arrested for contributing to the delinquency of minors.

Page and Clelland found that the most significant difference between the two factions was level of education. With regard to occupational and economic indicators, both groups were similar. The differences in educational level reflect the differences in life-style. Page and Clelland feel that the protesters were trying to protect a life-style—which they call "cultural fundamentalism"—that has been under attack throughout the twentieth century.

This cultural fundamentalism is reflected in concerns with the content of modern textbooks. Cultural fundamentalists object to textbooks that appear to show disrespect for God and the Bible, use vulgar language, support secular humanism, and, most important, show disrespect for authority. In Kanawha County, the cultural fundamentalists were most concerned with the writings of Mark Twain, George Bernard Shaw, and Norman Mailer because these authors were disrespectful of authority and institutionalized practices.

In the words of Page and Clelland, "Cultural fundamentalism was once the dominant life-style in the United States. Its strength has been eroded by such master trends as urban heterogeneity, consumer-oriented affluence, and the pervasive drive of rationalization in all spheres of life."[14]

School administrations in factional communities must learn to walk a political tightrope. At any moment, the community might be plunged into highly emotional conflict that would require the superintendent to attempt to reconcile both sides. In addition, because control of the school board might change, the superintendent cannot afford to take sides. From the standpoint of the school administrator, a factional community is one of the worst places to work. McCarty and Ramsey describe the superintendent in the factional community they studied as being so affected by the pressures of the job that he could barely light his cigarette at board meetings and was rapidly developing ulcers.

The most effective technique for a school administrator in a factional community is to avoid taking sides and remain as silent as possible on most issues. For instance, a superintendent should give the appearance of working hard for both factions. Both factions should think that he or she is on their side. Silence is the best rule for an administrator in major factional disputes; this avoids any appearance of taking sides. In addition, if the majority on a factional school board makes a decision, the superintendent should avoid giving whole-hearted support in case there is shift in power. Another recommendation is the creation of large committees composed of community members to study any potentially explosive educational issue. This allows any negative feelings on the part of board members to be directed at the committee and not the school administrators. Also, the large number of reports from these committees can diffuse the strong emotions surrounding the issue under consideration.

Figure 5.2 provides a summary of education decision making in a factional community. Factional power structures result in factional boards of education, which require superintendents who act as political strategists. The best political strategies include not favoring either faction, maintaining silence, balancing factions, and using committees extensively. School board debates depend on the nature of the factions and the faction in control of the board. Factional communities are noted for their high degree of conflict.

Pluralistic Communities

McCarty and Ramsey are full of praise for what they consider to be the ideal community power structure: pluralistic. In these communities they found model school boards and superintendents. The problem

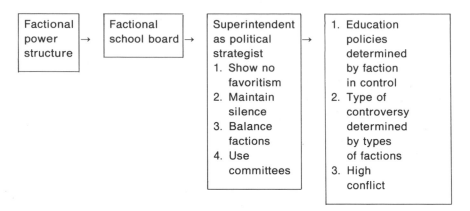

FIGURE 5.2 EDUCATIONAL POLICIES IN FACTIONAL COMMUNITY

with their praise, as William Boyd discusses in an insightful review of their study, is that these model boards and superintendents seem to exist only in stable, and often upper-middle-class, suburbs.[15] In our model, these communities are concerned about training their children to enter occupations that require a high level of schooling. Consequently, they focus on a college preparatory curriculum.

In McCarty and Ramsey's pluralistic community, the power structure had passed through a phase of domination by a single industry to a period of competition between groups. Unlike a factional community, no single group had ever gained a majority on the board of education. In this particular community, power was diffused through competition between an organized group of Catholics, two Protestant churches, the chamber of commerce, a labor union, and the PTA.[16]

These groups did not tend to form lasting coalitions. At the time the researchers entered the community, a bond issue was being opposed by Catholics, the chamber of commerce, and the labor union, and supported by the Protestant churches and the PTA. Regarding the elementary school report card, the PTA, the Catholic organization, and the two Protestant churches worked together to develop a progressive report card on which progress was measured against the potential learning of the student, as opposed to mastery of subject matter. Members of the chamber of commerce opposed the progressive report card because they believed employers needed an accurate record of a future employee's achievements.

The superintendent in this community played the role of professional adviser. He supported the bond issue in professional statements about the need for additional classrooms and more teachers. On the report card issue, he helped organize the committee and quoted research information on the effect of different report cards on student learning. In most situations, he acted as an expert who provided the board with information to aid in their decision making and faithfully administered their decisions.

McCarty and Ramsey argue that pluralistic communities are typically open-minded and rely on facts. On most major issues, community-wide investigative committees are established to report to the board of education and the administration. Boards of education in these communities, which they call "status-congruent," do not meddle in the administration of the schools, but are active in the formulation of policy. Status-congruent boards encourage open debate with the hope of reaching a consensus.

Interestingly, status-congruent boards are selected in a relatively closed system. McCarty and Ramsey claim that if selection to the board depends on the vote of the mass public, then candidates will be elected because they are identifiable representatives of special-interest groups. With status-congruent boards, members are selected in a caucus system and the actual voting is pro forma. The caucus system, they argue, limits the number of members who serve particular special interests and, consequently, reduces the possibility for developing factions on the board. Therefore, status-congruent boards tend to be self-perpetuating, with members chosen by a nominating caucus and elections rubber-stamping the caucus.

In performing the role of professional adviser to a status-congruent board, the superintendent moves cautiously to avoid adverse community reaction to proposals for change. He or she should not surprise the board or the community with any sudden new proposals. In addition, the superintendent should study each board member carefully to avoid any explosive situations. A superintendent in a status-congruent community will sometimes function as a decision maker. In these situations, he or she will surround him- or herself with expert administrative advisers. The role of superintendent may fluctuate from professonal adviser to decision maker, depending on the mood of the board of education.

Figure 5.3 summarizes educational policy development in a pluralistic community. The membership of the school board is controlled by a nominating caucus, with the superintendent functioning as a political adviser. Educational policies are the result of broad community investigations and professional advice.

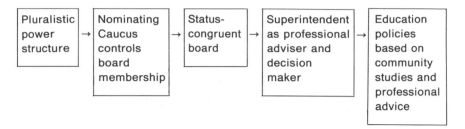

FIGURE 5.3 EDUCATIONAL POLICIES IN A PLURALISTIC COMMUNITY

Inert Communities

Finally, inert communities give the majority of power over school issues to the superintendent. In our model, the labor market in inert communities is not dependent on a high level of education. Most jobs in these communities are in agriculture and small factories. As McCarty and Ramsey describe them, inert communities are ideologically homogeneous, have no sense of purpose, and confine their energy to one community activity, such as trying to attract new industries. An inert community has no clear group structure, and most people follow an individualistic philosophy.

Within this community framework, it is difficult to get people to run for the school board. In most situations, the composition of the board is indirectly controlled by the superintendent. Board members turn to the superintendent for leadership and decision making. In some cases, McCarty and Ramsey report, the superintendent claimed that board members accepted 99 percent of his or her proposals. Very seldom in inert communities does the board turn to leaders outside the school system for advice on educational matters.

McCarty and Ramsey therefore call the board "sanctioning" because it primarily accepts the recommendations of the superintendent. In this situation, the "decision-making" superintendent assumes that the board will accept any reasonable recommendations, and he or she does not consult outside community leaders.

In an inert community studied by McCarty and Ramsey, the superintendent held his position for twenty-nine years and maintained firm control over the selection process for board elections. School board members reported that the superintendent always recommended to them names of candidates. In turn, board members would urge those the superintendent had selected to run for office. These candidates usually ran without any opposition. When nomination committees were used, the superintendent would recommend the names for membership.

In order to maintain his relationship with the board, the superintendent avoided any issue that might upset its members. Most of his activities were conducted behind the scenes by contacting board members about issues that were to be discussed before future meetings. Therefore, he knew how each member was planning to vote on a particular issue. In this manner, he could avoid confrontations.

McCarty and Ramsey found the actions of the superintendent typical of other inert communities. They conclude that the decision-making superintendent tries to avoid any controversy with the board, and between the board and community. The superintendent is aided by his influence over the selection of candidates for the board. An important method of control for this type of superintendent is the giving, withholding, and slanting of information about the school system to the board. In addition, the decision-making superintendent is the source of new ideas for change and refinement of educational policies. While working behind the scenes, the superintendent tries to assure open discussions at board meetings in order to give the members a feeling of freedom.

In *Growing Up American,* Alan Peshkin describes a rural Illinois community in which the primary educational concern is with the weekend football or basketball game.[17] Advanced educational training is of little importance to the needs of the local labor market. Of the approximately 360 full-time working men in the community, 240 work in factories, 90 in agriculture, and 33 in businesses. Women in the community are employed in equal proportions as clerks, factory workers, and secretaries. Within this economic context, Peshkin found the goal of the schools to be providing a good basic education.

Traditionally, the school board in this community has been composed of farmers and, with one exception, men. As in other communities of this type, the major responsibility for running the school system is given to the superintendent. During Peshkin's study of the community, the superintendent of seventeen years died and was replaced by a similar type of leader. Both superintendents acted as strong decision makers.

In Peshkin's words, the "school board prefers a strong superintendent who can run their schools, but this preference rests on a critical condition—that the superintendent perform in a manner that fits Mansfield."[18] In other words, the superintendent is the decision maker as long as she or he remains in tune with the community's values.

Peshkin sat in on the board's discussions of candidates for the superintendent's position. According to Peshkin, board members rejected candidates for having "big-city ideas," being "too intelligent for the community," having "too many ideas," and being "a little slow on discipline problems." They selected a superintendent who shared their values and background. They felt comfortable giving the decision-making power to this type of person.[19]

The role of the decision-making superintendent in a community with an inert power structure is summarized in Figure 5.4. The superintendent controls by influencing school board nominations, monitoring the flow of information about the school system to the board, avoiding controversy, and working behind the scenes with each board member. And finally, the superintendent initiates and controls most education policies.

It is important for the reader to remember that the application of any one of the four models depends on the type of power structure in the local community. Also, it is assumed that the nature of the community power structure determines the political style of the board of education and the school superintendent, and that these are all related to the community's occupational needs. A problem with these models is that they neglect the political power of educational bureaucracies and teachers' unions. The next two sections will integrate these political forces into the patterns of local governance.

EDUCATIONAL BUREAUCRACY

A large number of studies of local school politics stress the domination of educational policy making by the superintendent and local educational bureaucracy. In fact, William Boyd criticizes the study by McCarty and Ramsey because it emphasizes the importance of community power structures. In his review of the literature, Boyd writes: "Most research indicates that instead of being dominated by a powerful elite or being influenced by coalitions which shift with the issue ... local educational policy making is generally dominated by the influence of the top school administrators." Boyd argues that it is often difficult to discern where the power of the community ends and the power of school administrators begins. In many situations, Boyd argues, adminstrators act according to what they perceive to be the wishes of the community. Administrators are free to exert control over educational policies as long as they operate within the values and desires of the community. Boyd calls this the "zone of tolerance." In Boyd's words, "Since for pragmatic political reasons ... schoolmen usually seek to avoid conflict, it is unlikely that they will very often attempt to give the community other than what the community 'wants.' "[20] In another study, L. Harmon Zeigler and M. Kent Jennings

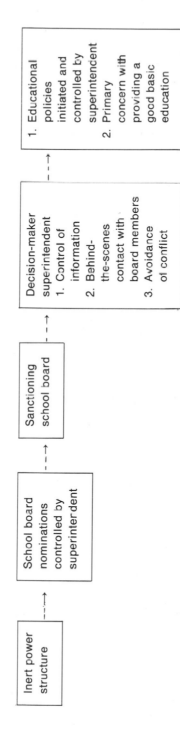

FIGURE 5.4 EDUCATIONAL POLICIES IN AN INERT COMMUNITY

The boxes, read in sequence, contain:

Inert power structure

School board nominations controlled by superintendent

Sanctioning school board

Decision-maker superintendent
1. Control of information
2. Behind-the-scenes contact with board members
3. Avoidance of conflict

1. Educational policies initiated and controlled by superintencent
2. Primary concern with providing a good basic education

found that the policy-making process of local school boards was controlled by superintendents.[21]

Obviously, the degree of administrative control is dependent on the nature of local school politics. In the four models discussed in the previous section, the superintendent assumes significant political power in pluralistic and inert communities. In dominated and factional communities, the superintendent is either the pawn of the power structure or an astute political strategist. For instance, school administrators were not in control of the political events in the previously discussed textbook controversy in Kanawha County, West Virginia.

Studies of communities controlled by educational administrators provide an analysis of the techniques and methods of administrative domination. In addition, many of these studies are critical of administrative control and blame many educational problems on the existence of rigid bureaucracies.

Certainly, the most widely recognized method of administrative control is the ability of superintendents to act as gatekeepers of information. Through this method, a superintendent can ensure that school board members receive only information that is favorable to his or her policies. In the words of Zeigler and Jennings, "A superintendent who occupies a gatekeeping position with respect to the flow of information to the board is ideally situated to select only what he wants the board to hear." And, according to their study, "Most observers acknowledge that many, if not all, superintendents occupy a strategic gatekeeping position, particularly where technical information is concerned."[22]

Through the gatekeeping of information, according to Zeigler and Jennings, superintendents are able to control the types of issues considered by school boards. In addition, the superintendent can define alternative methods of action. This gives the superintendent control of the major part of the policy-making arena. He or she determines for the board what is to be considered and how it is to be considered. Quoting one political scientist, Zeigler and Jennings write, "Consequently, the superintendent who controls issue definition indirectly controls the type of educational-political market within which policies are decided. As Schattsschneider once observed, 'The definition of the alternatives is the supreme instrument of power.'"[23]

Another method used by school administrators is to convince boards of education that only administrators have technical expertise in most areas of educational policy. In the twentieth century, this is a classic technique used by administrators to justify control of the policy-making process. The claim is made that educational decisions require expert opinion and that professional educators, and not elected board members, are the only people qualified to make those decisions. If elected school board members accept this argument, then they often defer to the expert opinion of the superintendent.

As part of the method of gatekeeping, superintendents often exercise control over the agenda for school board meetings. This ensures that only the issues the superintendent wants to be discussed will be discussed. In 70 percent of the school districts studied by Zeigler and Jennings, superintendents had primary control of the agenda and in two-thirds of the districts the superintendent had sole responsibility. Also, to build political support, superintendents rely on informal contacts with individual board members and spend time socializing new board members to district policies. In some cases, superintendents try to build their own political coalitions among community members.[24]

While the superintendent might control policy through gatekeeping, informal contacts, and community coalitions, the central office staff of the local school system also exercises a degree of control. These middle managers (associate and assistant superintendents, supervisors, and heads of special projects) generally resist any public input into the school system and try to maintain control over all educational policies in a local school system.

As discussed in Chapter 2, McGivney and Haught argue that the most important need of central office staff is to perceive itself in control of a situation. The desire to control a situation, they argue, has the greatest explanatory and predictive power with regard to the actions of the central office staff.[25] Also discussed in Chapter 2 is the tendency for educational bureaucracies to pursue policies that increase their salaries and job opportunities.

Like the superintendent, the gatekeeping of information is an important method of control for the central office staff. For instance, McGivney and Haught give examples of the efforts of the central office "to establish and maintain central control over communications to such agencies as city hall, the state education department, principals, and teachers, and other extra-school-system groups."[26]

With regard to control of the policy-making process, McGivney and Haught argue that a major role is played by informal networks within the central office bureaucracy. In their study, they found that the central office was divided into two major subgroups, with each subgroup composed of minor subgroups. Each subgroup met informally each day, with one subgroup being oriented toward the board of education and the other toward building principals and teachers. The location of offices played an important role in determining the membership of each subgroup. The actions of each of these subgroups were essential parts of the informal structure of power. The general pattern of decision making, according to McGivney and Haught, was for each subgroup to try to reach a consensus over an issue. A proposal accepted by a minor subgroup would be accepted by the major subgroups. McGivney and Haught found that proposals that were considered by the major subgroup without first receiving acceptance by a minor subgroup were delayed until they received that acceptance; and, they argue, "Proposals submitted in major subgroups by isolates will be either rejected or delayed."[27]

After going through this informal network of subgroups, a proposal is submitted to an administrative council for agreement by the whole central office. A proposal introduced into an administrative council without major subgroup approval is delayed until that action occurs. If consensus is reached in favor of a proposal by the central office staff, then it is sent to a school board study meeting for consideration. In the words of McGivney and Haught, the central office staff "utilizes the board's study session to produce a predictable vote for or against a proposal at the official board meeting."[28]

Over the years there has been a great deal of criticism of the power and control of educational bureaucracies. They have been accused of being insulated from community influences and of focusing most of their attention on internal struggles for power. Often, it is argued, members of an educational bureaucracy are more concerned with extrinsic rewards than with service to a client. Principals and teachers in the system are often faced with a multitude of often-contradictory statements coming from different parts of the bureaucracy, and the bureaucratic units are more concerned with their own prestige and advancement than with helping the schools. In his study of the New York City school bureaucracy, David Rogers writes, "These loyalties, cliques, and internal power struggles were an essential element in headquarters politics.... Predictably the divisions [within the school administration] competed in trying to secure larger shares of the scarce resources of the system. 'What will this do to our unit?' was the usual question when reforms were discussed."[29]

Educational bureaucracies tend to have the greatest power in urban and in large consolidated school districts. As Boyd states, "As the size of the school system increases, the visibility of lay opposition groups tends to decrease, and school system bureaucracy, the social distance to school authorities, and the ability of the system to maintain 'business as usual' in the face of lay opposition tends to increase."[30]

Therefore, in dominated and factional communities, educational bureaucracies have more power when the school district is large. For instance, a faction boycotting a school in an urban area will not have as much of an effect as a factional boycott in a small school district. In addition, ruling elites in urban areas might complain about their inability to change the local schools because of an entrenched bureaucracy.

Criticisms of educational bureaucracies reveal another aspect of the issue of control in local school districts. The issue is not the desire by bureaucracies to control, but the the inability of bureaucracies to change in response to outside demands. This issue cuts across every type of community power structure. In other words, a distinction should be made between educational bureaucracies that are in control and educational bureaucracies that are out of control.

As stated before, educational bureaucracies are most likely to be out of control in large, as opposed to small, school districts. And even if the superintendent and the central office give the appearance of exerting major control over local educational policies, there is still the possibility that they are acting within the range of community expectations, or what William Boyd calls the zone of tolerance.

TEACHERS' UNIONS

Teachers' union contracts have an important effect on policies in local school districts. Union contracts are often negotiated outside the range of direct public control. Therefore, teachers' unions can have an effect on school politics that is independent of the local community power structure. This condition is reflected in the wide variation of union practices that seem to operate independently of any particular type of community environment or power structure. In fact, it is difficult to generalize about the effect of teachers' unions on local school politics because of the wide variations in labor relationships. In *Teachers' Unions in the Schools*, Susan Moore Johnson writes about her study of local teachers' unions: "It would have been nice to have derived a simple, neatly predictive model to explain the great diversity in educational labor practices, but none was to be found."[31]

Johnson's study was limited to six communities, of which three were urban, one was suburban, one was a suburban consolidated district, and one was rural. Based on this limited sample, she concluded there is more trust and cooperation between unions and local school officials in smaller school districts. Communities with a strong local labor tradition are more supportive of teachers' unions. In addition, union negotiations are more difficult when there is a shortage of funds for local schools. Besides these rather commonsense conclusions, she was unable to provide a model that could be used to predict labor relations in a particular type of community.

Any discussion of the effect of local teachers' unions on school politics must therefore recognize wide variations in practice. These variations occur even when negotiated contracts contain similar language. According to Johnson, much of the variation is a result of individual personalities, personal relationships between school administrators and teachers, and teachers' attitudes towards their school and school system. She writes, "The experiences of these districts suggest that teachers and principals remake even this locally derived policy [union contract] until it is their own—until it is consistent with past practices and current preferences. Contract implementation, like program implementation, demands ongoing mutual adaptation between the rules and local school practices."[32]

Even with variations between school districts, there is an increasing trend for local teachers' union contracts to include policy matters along with wage settlements. The negotiation of noneconomic items has removed many policy discussions from the traditional arena of school politics. In fact, one of the important consequences of the expansion of noneconomic items in teachers' union contracts is the possible loss of public control. It can be argued that during negotiations, the public is represented by a board of education. The assumption is that the board functions as elected representatives of the public in bargaining with teachers' unions. A major problem with the argument is that boards of education tend not to play an active role in negotiations and give the majority of responsibility to either professional negotiators or members of the administrative staff.

In their study of trends in teachers' union contracts, McDonnell and Pascal think it is naive of the public to assume that a board of education plays a major role in union negotiations. They argue, "Citizens may simply assume that their elected representatives on the school board take an active part in negotiations, but we have seen that this rarely happens."[33] They found a lack of community participation in most contract negotiations and discovered that school boards were often divorced from negotiations except for approval of the final contract. In many districts, it was found, collective bargaining was being handled by a director of personnel and/or an employee in public relations. Consequently, one effect of labor negotiations is to strengthen control by school administrators and teachers over school district policies relative to school boards and the public.

McDonnell and Pascal found that since the early 1970s, items in teachers' union contracts have steadily expanded to include areas traditionally controlled by school administrators. For instance, items in some contracts now include teacher participation in the evaluation of other teachers, teacher supervision of other teachers, and the establishment of school building committees and grievance procedures. The last two items, grievance procedures and building committees, have helped teachers counter the power of school administrators. More general policy issues in some teachers' contracts include class size, working hours, number of faculty meetings, policy review committees, and textbook committees.[34] Susan Moore Johnson found the same range of contract provisions. In the six school districts in her study, contract items dealt with the following: grievance procedures, union privileges in schools, building committees, evaluations and ratings, personnel files, personal leave, lunch duty, meetings, extracurricular assignments, teacher assignments, length of workday, evening meetings, preparation periods, extra duties, teaching load, and class size.[35]

McDonnell and Pascal found that the noneconomic provisions in contracts had their greatest effect at the school building level. They write, "The noneconomic effects of collective bargaining are more perceptible at the school than the district level. Because of contractual provisions ... principals have less latitude than before in managing their own buildings."[36]

Union contracts have formalized and made more complex the internal governance of school systems. Charles Kerchner uses the term "multilateral" to describe the style of governance resulting from collective bargaining. He argues that the traditional hierarchical structure of schooling with a unitary command structure has broken down and been replaced with one that involves continuous negotiations between a variety of actors in a school system.[37]

Kerchner uses one incident in a California elementary school to depict both the changes in the command structure in education and the role of teacher building committees. In this particular school a group of vandals had entered over a weekend, destroying equipment and stealing the master key for all the classrooms. The teachers became concerned that the thieves could enter their classrooms and steal personal property. The principal called the central office to have the locks changed and received a firm refusal because of the expense. As Kerchner points out, before there was a union, that would have been the end of the issue. But in this case, the building representative for the California Teachers' Association got on the phone and told the central office that if they didn't change the locks there would be a major grievance. The locks were changed in a few days.[38]

Any general analysis of the effect of teachers' unions must consider the pursuit of the collective interests of teachers in relationship to other interests within a school district. For instance, demands for higher wages affect the amount of money that can be spent on other things. In addition, the pursuit of greater power for teachers conflicts with the interests of administrators in protecting their power.

Randall Eberts and Lawrence Pierce have looked at the effect of collective bargaining on the battle over resources in 1,336 school districts in Michigan and New York.[39] They feel that during periods of declining enrollments and budgets, school adminstrators have a number of options for dealing with the situations:

1. Administrators can decide not to fill vacant teaching positions.
2. They can defer any salary increase for teachers.
3. They can cut nonprofessional staff.
4. Expenses can be reduced by requiring teachers to teach more and larger classes, by reducing or eliminating teacher preparation periods, and by eliminating inservice.
5. Teaching supplies can be cut.
6. Older, more experienced teachers can be replaced with younger and cheaper teaching staff.

If one considers these options in light of union concerns, it is easy to see the possible effect of union demands on resource allocations and educational policy. For instance, unions would certainly fight against the option of replacing an older staff with a younger staff. In fact, most union contracts contain language protecting the seniority rights of teachers. Unions would also fight any attempt to defer salary increases for teachers. Protection of seniority rights and salaries is the most important priority of most unions and has been a major issue in most strikes. This would mean that with a strong union in a district school, authorities would have to select other means for reducing the budget. Most teachers' unions would fight against larger class sizes and the elimination of teacher preparation periods, but these issues would not have as high a priority as salaries and job protection; no teachers' union has conducted a strike just over class size and preparation periods. Indeed, it is hard to imagine a teachers' union striking because of a hiring freeze, the cutting of nonprofessional staff, or a reduction in supplies.[40]

In other words, as Eberts and Pierce found in their study, the existence of a strong union has a major impact on decisions about the allocation of resources. Given the goals and structure of teachers' unions, their primary concern is to protect jobs and seniority rights and to increase wages. Unions will tend to resist any educational policies that threaten those primary concerns.

Not only do the collective interests of strong teachers' unions affect resource allocations and educational policies, but they also threaten the interests of school administrators. As teachers' unions gain more power, they reduce the power of other school administrators.

In fact, one complaint of school principals is that their interests are often not represented during collective bargaining sessions. Susan Moore Johnson recorded complaints by principals about the impact of contract provisions on local schools. In one community, she reported, "there were principals who objected that teachers had been granted a duty-free lunch without the provision of cafeteria aides to supervise students." In another community, principals complained of the vagueness of contract language regarding supervision of preparation periods.[41]

The most dramatic example of the struggle for power between administrators and teachers' unions occurred in 1987 in Rochester, New York, when the local administrators' union filed suit against the local teachers' union over its mentor teacher program. The suit contained objections similar to those raised the previous year by administrators in New York City against a master teacher program. The argument in both situations was that the programs gave teachers duties and power that were normally part of the job of principals and assistant principals.

In Rochester, the mentor teacher program was agreed on in collective bargaining sessions between the Rochester Teachers' Association (AFT) and the school district. The program relieves some teachers of teaching duties so that they can help improve the skills of first-year teachers and tenured teachers who are having difficulties.

The suit filed by the Association of Supervisors and Administrators of Rochester claimed that the mentor teachers were performing administrative and supervisory tasks without proper state credentials. The head of the administrators' association, Patricia Carnahan, stated, "As far as I am concerned, this program encroaches on the jobs of those currently involved in the evaluation process.... The district and teachers' union are saying that evaluations of new teachers done by administrators are to be shared with the panel [includes mentor teachers], and we are saying 'no.'" Similar objections were raised by Ted Elsberg, president of the Council of Supervision and Administration of the City of New York. He objected to the creation of the position of master teacher, who would perform functions similar to those of the mentor teachers in Rochester, because the role already existed in the schools in the form of principals and assistant principals. What he wanted was for the city to hire 200 new assistant principals. Arthur Wise, director of the RAND Corporation's Center for the Study of the Teaching Profession, stated in reference to the court action, "I think these are perhaps the first signs of administrative resistance to the emerging idea of teacher professionalism.... Unfortunately, we will probably be seeing more of this."[42]

Therefore, while it is difficult to generalize about the effect of teachers' unions on local school districts because of the wide variations in practice, where teachers' unions are strong they do affect local school district policies and resource allocations, and create power struggles with local administrators. Often, unions work outside the normal channels of community power. Like any union organization, they are primarily concerned with the collective interests of their members. These interests include enhancing teacher power, increasing wages, and protecting jobs.

CONCLUSION

Local educational politics varies according to the type of community power structure, the nature of the local labor market, the power of the local educational bureaucracy, and the militancy of the local teachers' union. While these variations exist between school districts, a great deal of uniformity is imposed on local schools by state and federal educational policies. In fact, one can argue that local political battles are of little importance when compared to those that occur in state and federal politics.

An often-heard plea is to restore local control of the schools. It is not very clear what this would accomplish. In the past, local control of schools often meant control by local power elites who discriminated against the poor and minority groups. It required political activity by civil rights groups to gain federal intervention to end discrimination by local school systems. Those who argue for local control might simply be advocating restoring power to these local elites.

On the other hand, local control of schools might free them from the constantly changing educational policies that result from state and federal politics. With greater local control, local school policies would not be linked to changes in national administrations or foreign policy. But, of course, greater local control might bring about local educational policies that change to meet the needs of local business interests. In many ways, the choice might be between the uncertainties and change of federal intervention, and the possibility of discrimination by local elites. As in any political issue, there is no easy solution.

In summary, the following list contains factors that must be considered in analyzing local educational politics. The list should be considered in the context of the discussions of each of the items in this chapter. Given the wide range of communities in the United States, there is no necessary relationship between these various factors. For instance, a community could have a dominated type of power structure that is constantly frustrated by the intransigence of the local school bureaucracy. On the other hand, the same type of power structure might operate in a community in which the bureauracy is easily controlled.

While communities in the United States vary widely, they share certain patterns. As argued in the first part of this chapter, the educational requirements of the local labor market often determine the type of power structure, which, in turn, determines the governing style of the superintendent. Dominated power structures tend to exist in communities with a single industry or a diversified labor market, and they tend to have dominated school boards and functionary superintendents. The educational needs of the labor market are of little concern in a factional community, which tends to have a factional school board and a superintendent who is a political strategist. Pluralistic communities are often oriented towards labor markets that require a college education, and they tend to have status-congruent school boards with superintendents who act like professional advisers. In inert communities, the local labor market usually requires a minimal level of education, and the school board tends to be sanctioning, with a decision-maker type of superintendent. In addition, teacher's unions and school bureaucracies tend to have more power and influence in larger school districts.

Again, the reader is cautioned that, in spite of these patterns, each community should be analyzed according to each factor in the following list.

Factors in Local Politics of Education

1. Nature of community power structure
   a. dominated
   b. factional
   c. pluralistic
   d. inert
2. Educational needs of the local labor market
   a. diversified
   b. single-industry
   c. suburban community (primary interest in preparation for college)
   d. Rural, small-town, or suburban (minimum educational concerns for future employment)
3. Governing style of school board
   a. dominated
   b. factional

  c. status-congruent
  d. sanctioning
4. Governing style of superintendent
  a. functionary
  b. political strategist
  c. professional adviser
  d. decision maker
5. Power of educational bureaucracy
  a. operating in zone of tolerance
  b. in control of policies
  c. out of control
6. Power of teachers' union
  a. range of noneconomic items in contract
  b. effect of contract on allocation of resources
  c. conflict with local administrators
  d. Participation of union in politics of local school boards

NOTES

1. For a general discussion of the development of magnet schools, see Kathy Borman and Joel Spring, *Schools in Central Cities* (White Plains, N.Y.: Longman, 1984), pp. 160–72.
2. Donald McCarty and Charles Ramsey, *The School Managers: Power and Conflict in American Public Education* (Westport, Conn.: Greenwood, 1971).
3. Ibid., pp. 27–79.
4. David Kirby, T. Robert Harris, and Robert Crain, *Political Strategies in Northern School Desegregation* (Lexington, Mass.: Lexington Books, 1973), p. 84.
5. See Michael Timpane, *Corporations and Public Education*, a report distributed by Teachers College, Columbia University (May 1981), p. 34; and *Chicago United and the Chicago Board of Education* (March 1981), a report distributed by Chicago United. A general discussion of this relationship can be found in Borman and Spring, *Schools in Central Cities*, pp. 183–86.
6. For a discussion of these political changes, see Joseph Cronin, *The Control of Urban Schools* (New York: Free Press, 1973), pp. 39–123; Joel Spring, *Education and the Rise of the Corporate State* (Boston: Beacon Press, 1972), pp. 85–135; and David Tyack, *The One Best System* (Cambridge, Mass.: Harvard University Press, 1974), pp. 126–67.
7. Willis D. Hawley, *Nonpartisan Elections and the Case for Party Politics* (New York: John Wiley, 1973).
8. *The Boston Compact: An Operational Plan for Expanded Partnerships with the Boston Public Schools, September 1982*, booklet distributed by the Boston public school system.
9. "A Community of Believers," in *The Atlanta Partnership of Business &*

Education, Inc.: Second Anniversary Report, undated booklet distributed by the Atlanta Partnership of Business & Education.

10. McCarty and Ramsey, *School Managers,* pp. 79–127.
11. Ibid., pp. 87–97.
12. Ibid., p. 97.
13. Ann L. Page and Donald A. Clelland, "The Kanawha County Textbook Controversy: A Study of the Politics of Life-Style Concern, "*Social Forces,* Vol. 57, No. 1 (September 1978), 265–68.
14. Ibid., p. 276.
15. William Boyd, "The Public, the Professionals, and Educational Policy Making: Who Governs?," *Teachers College Record,* Vol. 77, No. 4, (May 1976), 547–49.
16. McCarty and Ramsey, *School Manager,* pp. 127–43.
17. Alan Peshkin, *Growing Up American: Schooling and the Survival of Community* (Chicago: University of Chicago Press, 1978), p. 10.
18. Ibid., p. 58.
19. Ibid., pp. 74–82.
20. Boyd, "The Public, the Professionals," p. 548, 551–52.
21. L. Harmon Zeigler and M. Kent Jennings, *Governing American Schools: Political Interaction in Local School Districts* (North Scituate, Mass.: Duxbury Press, 1974).
22. Ibid., p. 189.
23. Ibid., p. 189.
24. Ibid., pp. 190–94.
25. Joseph H. McGivney and James M. Haught, "The Politics of Education: A View from the Perspective of the Central Office Staff," *Educational Administration Quarterly,* Vol. 8, No. 3 (August 1972), 35.
26. Ibid., p. 23.
27. Ibid., p. 30.
28. Ibid.
29. David Rogers, *110 Livingston Street: Politics and Bureaucracy in the New York City Schools* (New York: Random House, 1968), p. 301.
30. Boyd, "The Public, the Professionals," p. 560.
31. Susan Moore Johnson, *Teachers' Unions in the Schools* (Philadelphia: Temple University Press, 1984), p. 169.
32. Ibid., p. 172.
33. Lorraine McDonnell and Anthony Pascal, *Organized Teachers in American Schools* (Santa Monica, Calif.: Rand Corporation, 1979), p. 87.
34. Ibid., pp. 1–90.
35. Johnson, *Teachers' Unions,* pp. 190–211.
36. McDonnell and Pascal, *Organized Teachers,* p. ix.
37. Charles T. Kerchner, "Unions and Their Impact on School Governance and Politics," in Anthony M. Cresswell and Michael Murphy, eds., *Teachers, Unions, and Collective Bargaining in Public Education* (Berkeley, Calif.: McCutchan, 1980), pp. 382–87.
38. Ibid., pp. 384–85.
39. Randall W. Eberts and Lawrence C. Pierce, *The Effects of Collective*

Bargaining in Public Schools (Eugene, Oreg.: Center for Educational Policy and Management, 1980).

40. Originally, I made this argument in Borman and Spring, *Schools in Central Cities*, pp. 134–59.
41. Johnson, *Teachers' Unions*, pp. 33–36.
42. Blake Rodman, "New York Lawsuit Highlights Growing Tension between Principals, Teachers over Their Roles," *Education Week*, Vol. 6, No. 16 (January 14, 1987), 1, 22.

CHAPTER 6

The Knowledge Industry

Textbooks and standardized tests convey the idea that what is taught in schools is neutral and that all scholars agree about what kinds of knowledge are valuable. Of course, nothing could be further from the truth. In every field of study, scholars disagree about content, interpretation, and methodology. In addition, most subject matter areas contain values and assumptions that conflict with the values and beliefs of some public group. Knowledge is not neutral, and the knowledge taught in schools is the result of political and economic decisions.

There are three components to the politics of knowledge: First, there is the politics of the curriculum, which includes decisions about what subjects to teach in the public schools. Second, there is the politics of content, which deals with what is to be taught in each subject. Last, there is the politics of testing, which includes decisions about what students ought to have learned.

The preceding chapters have focused on the politics of the curriculum. For instance, national education policies have dictated the teaching of particular subjects. During the Cold War period of the 1950s, science, mathematics, and foreign languages were emphasized, while in the 1960s, priorities shifted to the needs of disadvantaged children. In the 1970s, emphasis was placed on career and vocational subjects to reduce unemployment. During the 1980s, arguments for higher academic requirements arose because of concerns with international trade.

The politics of content primarily deals with the organization of the textbook industry, court decisions regarding textbooks, state laws, and the political and economic forces that affect publishing decisions. For most elementary and secondary students, a textbook is the major source of knowledge about a particular school subject. As we shall see, decisions about the content of textbooks are made in a very heated and political environment.

Since the accountability movement of the 1970s, standardized test scores have become the major method by which schools tell the public what and how much students have learned. When test scores are high, newspaper headlines declare the triumph of local schools; and when scores are low, they announce that the schools have failed. Some school systems use test scores to measure the effectiveness of teachers and principals.

The result is the tyranny of testing. Any school system that reports test scores to the public, and any teacher or principal whose effectiveness is measured according to student scores, must, out of self-interest, "teach for the test." Thus the content of standardized tests has a direct impact on what is taught in the classroom.

Standardized tests also foster the idea that all knowledge is neutral. For instance, it is difficult to defend the idea of "standardized" knowledge in controversial areas of study such as history, economics, government, and other social sciences. In any society that claims to allow freedom of ideas, it is difficult to create standardized tests. For instance, what are the most important things to be learned in social studies and literature, and therefore measured on nationally standardized tests? Who would be presumptuous enough to make that decision? In the United States, testing companies presume to decide such things, and school systems agree to accept their decisions. Testing companies are motivated by profit, and school districts are motivated by the desire for an instrument that can easily measure the supposed effectiveness of administrators and teachers.

In describing the politics of knowledge, we shall discuss first the issue of the neutrality of knowledge and the attitudes of the courts; then we shall move on to the politics of publishing and testing. The publishing and testing industries are money-making enterprises that operate in a politically controlled market. Consequently, both industries will have to be considered in their economic and political context.

THE MYTH OF NEUTRAL KNOWLEDGE

Professional educators, government officials, the publishing industry, and testing corporations help to perpetuate the myth of neutral knowledge. In this context, *neutral knowledge* refers to a universally agreed-upon standardized body of knowledge in a particular subject area. For instance, to avoid a loss of sales owing to controversies over content, publishers make their textbooks appear to present neutral knowledge. Being primarily interested in profits, the publishing industry tries to please all customers by avoiding any possible conflict over content. The avoidance of controversy often results in bland textbooks.

Professional educators and government officials also foster the idea of neutral knowledge when they report student learning in standardized test scores, as opposed to the content of what students have learned. Communities are told that their students have scored above grade level on standardized tests in mathematics and reading, but are never told what their students have learned. Even standardized test scores have no substantive meaning for most people. What does it mean to read at grade level? Since grade level is an artificial construct, the idea that all students should have mastered a given body of knowledge at a particular grade level is also artificial. But in order for educators and officials to gain professional acceptance, and in order for the public to accept the use of standardized tests, everyone concerned must act as if there really is such a uniform body of knowledge.

In addition, the size and bureaucratic organization of public schooling promotes uniformity of content in classrooms. The use of only one textbook in a given classroom or grade creates the impression that there is a body of standardized knowledge. Most schools require the use of a particular text in a classroom, while others require the use of the same textbook in all classrooms of a particular grade. Thus the public schools present a smaller variety of books and ideas than do commercial bookstores.

It can be argued that the uniformity of subject matter in the public schools gives students the impression that an agreed-upon body of standard knowledge exists in every discipline. If this were true, then public schools would be educating people to accept the idea later in life that school knowledge is neutral.

In addition, court decisions regarding the content of public-school instruction have focused on the constitutional issues of interference with the free exercise of religion and the establishment of religion. Consequently, the only major court challenges to the neutrality of knowledge presented in public schools have come from religious groups. In most situations, this means that a student or parent can object only on religious grounds to ideas taught in the public schools.

The courts' limited involvement in these matters has created the public impression that the only legitimate legal challenges must involve religious issues. The issues that appear in the popular press deal primarily with creationism versus evolution and differences over moral instruction. In fact, court decisions dealing with the censorship of books by school officials have assumed that political neutrality can exist in the selection process. Seldom, if ever, are there court challenges over political and economic teachings outside the context of religion. Within this framework, the content of public-school instruction appears to be neutral, except in the area of religious beliefs. The issues surrounding the content of public instruction can be illustrated by testimony given before the Texas State Textbook Committee and by court decisions.

Testimony given before the Texas commissioner of education and the State Textbook Committee shows how value-laden school knowledge can be. For many years, the policy of statewide adoption of textbooks in Texas has strongly influenced the publishing industry. Not wanting to lose big sales in Texas, publishers have paid close attention to the testimony given before the Texas State Textbook Committee and to its decisions.

Testimony before the committee highlights some of the subtle, but significant, meanings in small changes in wording in textbooks. For instance, consider the 1986 testimony of conservative textbook critic Mel Gabler regarding secondary-level texts on U.S. government. Having spent many years criticizing textbooks in all parts of the United States, Gabler and his wife are always vigilant for any sign of anti-Americanism, attacks on free-enterprise economics, and suggestions that federal controls might be needed to protect the environment.

Gabler complained to the committee about how many textbooks have treated the American Revolution. From his perspective, the War for Independence was not a revolution but an instance of colonial obedience to British law. As Gabler argued before the committee, "In other words, the colonists were obeying the laws. Actually, it was parliament that was breaking the law. Parliament was passing laws contrary to the British rights, the British Constitution." [1]

The way in which U.S. history is interpreted in the public schools profoundly affects the way in which American students view their country. An interpretation that presents the colonial break with Britain as revolutionary creates the image of the United States as the first modern revolutionary power and as a leader of democratic revolutions in the rest of the world. Gabler's interpretation creates an image of a nation of law-abiding citizens whose primary concern was with the protection of rights under a system of laws. These two views of American history have striking implications for the conduct of foreign policy, the shaping of American attitudes toward other nations, and the development of political culture.

Directly related to the issue of neutral knowledge is the Texas law requiring texts for grades seven through twelve to advocate the free-enterprise system. In Gabler's language, the law requires books to be "unneutral." In reference to this law, Gabler complained of a text that "treats agricultural problems, on a number of pages, as something to be solved by government, rather than as problems that government helped to create by interfering with the free market." [2]

Obviously, students' ideas about economic and political problems can be shaped according to the way in which the sources of economic problems are identified and described. Certainly, the source of economic problems in agriculture is open to debate. It is also debatable whether or not America's prosperity has been solely the result of free enterprise. Since the early days of the nineteenth century, the federal government has been involved in financing roads, building railroads, managing the financial system, and helping business to accumulate capital. Whether or not government interference has been a key element in economic development is therefore open to debate. But this area of dispute is not recognized by the Texas textbook law. Essentially, Texas law defines what knowledge about economics should be standard.

Important issues also arise in subjects less controversial than history and government. Consider the testimony of Jane Boyd of the National Organization for Women on the content of basal readers. Boyd explained to the committee that "My review of the basal readers for Grade 1 is primarily concerned with the equal representation of positive role models for both boys and girls." In her testimony she complained that "Three of the four basal readers under review at this time practice a form of sexism that makes invisible the possible triumphs that girls and women can experience." [3] More specifically, she directed the attention of the committee members to a story about a toad and a frog, both male, who "experience winter and independence together." She recommended that one of the characters be made female. [4] Changing the gender of the frog or toad would create a different image of appropriate sex-role behavior in the minds of students.

On a more humorous note, Suzanne Steinbach, a dictician, complained before the committee that an environmental studies text threatened the livestock industry by claiming that "Americans eat large quantities of beef. The conversion efficiency of plant material to beef is low. Is there any way to justify this kind of diet?" [5]

Obviously, such considerations make any subject taught in schools controversial. In addition, state textbook laws, like the one requiring advocacy of free enterprise, generate debate about whether or not the material is in violation of state law. State laws on the content of textbooks make it possible to raise objections about a wide variety of issues. Consider the Texas law stating that "Textbooks shall not contain certain material which serves to undermine authority." On the basis of this law, Lee Gaynier, a nurse, raised objections to a health book's definition of euthanasia because it made the act seem palatable. Gaynier reasoned, "Taking someone's life intentionally is murder. Murder is illegal. The book is teaching that murder is acceptable under certain circumstances, which is in violation of the General Content Requirement and Limitations [on undermining authority]." [6]

While testimony before the Texas Textbook Committee points up the controversial nature of knowledge, the greatest challenge to the neutrality of school knowledge has occurred in court cases brought by Protestant fundamentalists. These groups have rejected most public-school textbooks, as was discussed in the West Virginia case in the previous chapter, because textbooks lack religious content and do not recognize the authority of God. From the standpoint of these groups, if a textbook does not tell a student to seek answers for personal problems form the Bible or from some other religious source, then it is antireligious. The same charge is made if the textbook teaches something contrary to a fundamentalist interpretation of the Bible such as the theory of evolution.

On the other hand, school authorities have resisted complaints from religious groups about textbooks with the argument that it is necessary to have a uniform system of instruction and textbooks. This was the defense used by school officials in *Mozert v. Hawkins Public Schools* (1986), when religious groups objected to the content of the 1983 edition of the Holt, Rinehart & Winston reading series. According to the final decision rendered by Judge Thomas Hull, local public-school officials argued that "to permit individual teachers, students, parents, or ministers to choose the textbook of their liking would inescapably result in widespread chaos not only within the Hawkins County School System but also within the State of Tennessee." [7]

In the Mozert case, the plaintiffs complained that the content of the textbook series was inconsistent with their religious beliefs. Specifically, the plaintiffs believed "after reading the entire Holt series, a child might adopt the views of a feminist, a humanist, a pacifist, an anti-Christian, a vegetarian, or an advocate of a 'one-world government.'"

The major limitation in this type of case is that the issues must be related to religion. The only part of the U.S. Constitution that concerns objections to the content of instruction is the Free-Exercise Clause of the First Amendment, which prohibits the government from interfering with the free exercise of religion. In the case of the public schools, the schools are prohibited from requiring students to do anything that will interfere with the practice of their religion.

Arguing in the context of the Free-Exercise Clause of the First Amendment, the court required the Hawkins County schools to provide the plaintiff's children with alternative reading material. In the Mozert case, the court defined a two-step process for determining a free-exercise claim. The first step is to determine whether government action places a burden on the exercise of religion and whether that burden is balanced by a compelling government interest. The second step is to determine "whether the beliefs are religious and whether they are sincerely held by the individual asserting them." In the Mozert case, the court decided that the plaintiffs were arguing from a sincere religious position and that the government's interest in maintaining uniformity in textbooks was not a sufficient reason for interfering with the plaintiff's free exercise of religion.

In addition to their concern with the free exercise of religion, the courts have used the Free-Speech Clause of the First Amendment to establish a standard for the selection of school books. This standard assumes that the free speech of students is violated only when clearly stated political opinions guide the selection process.

The standard for the politically neutral selection of texts was established in *Board of Island Union Free School v. Steve A. Pico (1982)*, which involved the removal of books from the school library by the board of education because it believed that the contents of the books were unsuitable for high school students.[8] The case originated when several members of the board of education attended a conference of a politically conservative organization of parents concerned with educational legislation in New York State. While they were at the conference, the board members received a list of books considered morally and politically inappropriate for students. Upon returning from the conference, the board members investigated the contents of their high school library and ordered the removal of nine books that were on the list.

In rendering its decision, the U.S. Supreme Court recognized the power of school boards to select books and argued for the limitation of judicial interference in the operation of school systems. On the other hand, the Court recognized its obligation to guarantee that public institutions do not suppress ideas. In this particular case, it argued, there was a clear intention to suppress ideas by removing books contained in a list from a political organization.

The Court balanced the right of school boards to select books against the protection of the free speech of students by arguing that the decisions about selection could not be based on partisan or political motives. In the words of the Court, "If a Democratic school board, motivated by party affiliation, ordered the removal of all books written by or in favor of Republicans, few would doubt that the order violated the constitutional rights of the students denied access to those books." In another illustration, the Court argued, "The same conclusion would surely apply if an all-white school board, motivated by racial animus, decided to remove all books authored by blacks or advocating racial equality and integration."

While the Supreme Court decision was limited to the removal of books from the school library, it did establish a general standard for judging the actions of school officials regarding the content of books. The decision gave clear recognition to the power of school boards to select books. It also denied the right of school boards to select books according to a particular, and clearly recognized, political agenda. This standard does not preclude the possibility of the school board selecting books that might be ideologically offensive to some members of the community, unless, of course, the books intefere with the free exercise of religion.

In summary, the examples from testimony before the Texas State Textbook Committee illustrate how unneutral the content of most school textbooks is. Knowledge in most areas of study is debatable by scholars and by those with differing ideological positions. The only protection for the free speech of students is against texts that interfere with the free exercise of religion or against texts that have been selected according to a clear political agenda. Otherwise, school authorities, including school boards and state governments, have the right to select textbooks and require that they be read by students. In addition, states have the right to pass laws requiring that textbooks advocate the free-enterprise system or do not undermine authority. Clearly, these state laws advocate an ideological position, but one that has not been tested under the standard established in *Board of Island Union Free District v. Steven A. Pico.*

THE TEXTBOOK INDUSTRY

To understand how political forces determine the content of textbooks, one must examine the structure of the textbook industry. Most textbook publishers produce books that are not innovative and that reflect a politically conservative perspective. For instance, the very structure of the textbook industry works against innovation and creativity. Since its primary goal is to make a profit, the industry avoids risk by concentrating on mainstream textboks. This reluctance to take risks is due, in part, to the small number of companies in control of the textbook market. In 1986, the consolidation of the textbook industry increased with the sale by CBS of its publishing arm—which included Holt, Rinehart & Winston—to Harcourt Brace Jovanovich. This made Harcourt Brace Jovanovich the largest publisher of textbooks for elementary and secondary schools in the country. Also, during the same period, Time bought Scott, Foresman, and Company.[9]

These sales gave seven companies control of about 80 percent of the textbook market. Four of the seven are owned by larger corporations —for example, Gulf and Western owns Simon & Schuster and Prentice-Hall; and Time owns Little, Brown, Time-Life Books, and Scott, Foresman. The only three independent firms of the top seven publishing houses are Addison-Wesley, Macmillan, and Houghton Mifflin.[10]

At the time of the consolidation, it was generally believed that these larger companies would force the remaining small companies out of the market. The larger companies were planning to offer textbooks in every area rather than specialize in particular subjects. An article in *Education Week* states, "Small houses will have their place in the new textbook market only if the large companies specialize in a particular curricular area, as they did in the 1960s."[11]

Most students of the textbook industry agree that consolidation results in less innovation and a decline in quality. In the most extensive sociological study to date of the publishing industry, Lewis Coser, Charles Kadushin, and Walter Powell, argue that periods of high concentration in the publishing industry produce creative stagnation. One reason is that larger firms prefer "predictability, routine, and control, both for economic and for psychological reasons. Firms in concentrated industries, by virtue of their market power, feel no need to risk innovation even though customers might be interested in new products."[12]

In addition, in a small firm an ambitious project requires only a decision by a small group of people, while in a large firm the decision must go through an extensive chain of command, with each level of command acting cautiously. Coser, Kadushin, and Powell quote Townsend Hoopes, president of the Association of American Publishers: "the most fundamental measure of the health and vigor [of book publishing] is the number of active firms in the industry."[13]

Because of the desire of publishing houses for predictability and sure profits, their books are very similar in appearance and content. The reason is that publishers must rely on the success of previous publications to determine sales of new books. There is no method that accurately predicts the needs of the textbook market. Consequently, editors often examine the leading textbooks in the field to determine the type of book they want written. Very often, editors want a new textbook to resemble the leading seller in the field, but to contain some new features that make it slightly different. Consequently, particularly in a market dominated by only a few firms, all the books in a given subject matter area look pretty much alike. Of course, this does not mean that a different type of text might not sell. What it means is that publishers are afraid to risk publishing a textbook outside the common mold. Thus the textbook market continually reproduces look-alike texts that might in fact sell only because of the lack of competition.[14]

In fact, one of the major roles of acquisition editors is to help authors shape their prospective texts to fit the needs of the marketplace. What this means in practice is shaping the book to fit the content of the course as it is supposedly taught in most schools. Of course, this is difficult because no one knows exactly what is taught in courses across the nation, and the content of courses is often determined by textbooks. In the end, editors must rely on the content of existing textbooks to determine course content. After fitting the book to meet course content, acquisition editors then compare the prospective text to existing texts.

In addition, publishers rely on an "invisible college" of reviewers in making publishing decisions. Before publication, a company sends copies of the manuscript to several reviewers. These reviewers are selected from the contacts publishing houses make in the public schools and academic world. Most often, these reviewers are leading scholars in the field and are themselves authors of books.[15] By the time the process of comparison and review is completed, the acquisition editor has shaped a product that resembles other products in the field.

There is the possibility that this publishing process has perpetuated the content and structure of certain courses. Consider the possibility that textbooks largely determine the content of classroom teaching. If this is true, then the inherently conservative process of textbook acquisition and marketing causes the same material to be used in classrooms year after year. Thus any hope that some have of changing public schools depends on changes in the organization of the textbook industry.

Fear of censorship and of attack by pressure groups also makes publishers less willing to take risks. Publishers live in dread that an organized group will object to the content of their textbooks. Any sign of opposition to a particular text can make local school officials decide not to adopt it.

The Harold Rugg story exemplifies the difficulties faced by a textbook publisher when it publishes anything that does not reflect a consensus viewpoint. The story also demonstrates that even when textbooks are successful in the marketplace and widely accepted in the public schools, they can still be destroyed by attacks from special-interest groups.

During the 1930s, it is estimated that nearly half the social studies students in the United States used Harold Rugg's social science textbook series.[16] Rugg's major goal in the series was to overcome what he called the "impasse in citizenship." "The impasse," he writes, "has been frequently revealed by indifference to matters of public concern and by lack of trained intelligence on the part of the rank and file of our people to deal with their collective affairs." Rugg believed that citizens act from impulse rather than deliberative judgment and that the goal of organized social studies programs should be to train future citizens to apply intelligent judgment to major political, economic, and social problems. In Rugg's words, "Knowledge about the issue of contemporary life and how they came to be what they are could be translated into tendencies to act intelligently upon them, provided the machinery of the social studies is properly organized."[17]

In *America Revised: History Schoolbooks in the Twentieth Century*, Frances Fitzgerald writes about Rugg's success: "Harold Rugg's social-studies series for elementary-junior-high-school students ... was in many ways the crowning achievement of the progressive-education movement in the field of textbooks; it was, in fact, a democratic history—a history of the common man."[18] His series of social studies texts was not radical in the sense of being Marxist, but it did portray many of the difficulties and failures in American society. During a period of racial intolerance, the books promoted racial understanding and social justice. Rugg also advocated national economic planning and included problems related to unemployment, immigrants, and consumerism.

Protests against the Rugg series began in 1939. The Advertising Federation of America attacked the series for making negative statements about advertising. Cries of "socialist" and "communist" were heard from the National Association of Manufacturers, the American Legion, and newspapers. Local school boards banned the texts from the classroom because of attacks from many pressure groups. Rugg was forced to tour the country to defend his books against charges of communism and socialism. But there was little he could do about the attacks. School boards and public-school teachers shied away from using the books because of the potential of being drawn into the controversy. Fitzgerald reports that in 1938 Rugg's books sold 289,000 copies and that by 1944 the number had dropped to 21,000 copies.[19]

The decline of the Rugg textbook series is a classic example of the power pressure groups have over the textbook industry. Interestingly, one scholar of political socialization attributes the fact that high school civics courses have no effect on students' political values to the blandness of textbooks. In *Socialization to Politics*, Dean Jaros writes that as a result of community pressure on teachers and the blandness of textbooks, civics courses make little or no impression on students. He states, "Probably in response to pressure—real or imagined—from influential groups in society, teachers may avoid discussion of all but the most consensual community and regime-level values." Because of these real or imagined pressures, Jaros continues, "Most teachers, often abetted by the texts that they use, strike poses of explicit political neutrality." As a result, "teachers fail to communicate the fact that public policy involves social conflict and the resolution of different value positions." [20]

Political pressures can originate from a variety of sources. At the 1986 meeting of the Texas State Textbook Committee, there was testimony from groups ranging from the National Organization of Women to People for the American Way. People for the American Way represents an interesting type of pressure group because it was specifically organized to counter the actions of the religious right. Before the 1986 hearings of the textbook committee, Michael Hudson, director and general counsel of People for the American Way in Texas, stated the purpose of the 250,000-member national organization was to ensure that content changes in textbooks are "based on sound academic educational criteria and are not based on sectarian or political bias, as we feel has been the case sometimes in past years." Hudson went on to attack complaints about terms used in textbooks like "values clarification" and "decision making." He told the committee, "Moreover, these are religious-right catchwords or code words that have been used for years across not only Texas but across the entire nation to object to content that is somehow inconsistent with a particular and narrow religious or political viewpoint." [21]

In addition to their fear of pressure groups, textbook publishers are influenced by state adoption policies. For instance, fifteen states adopt textbooks on a statewide basis. The largest of these states, California, represents 11 percent of the textbook market. In the late 1970s, Bill Honig, then a member of the California State Board of Education and later state superintendent of instruction, was made aware of the state's power over the publishing industry. At a textbook hearing in California in 1977, Honig recalls making a casual comment about the television series "The Adams Chronicle." He suggested off the top of his head that students should know about Abigail Adams. "Sure enough," Honig writes, "in 1982, when the new batch of history books came up for adoption, almost every single major publisher had an insert on Abigail Adams." [22]

After learning that political power could be exerted over the textbook industry, Honig made it an important part of his political strategy for changing American education. He writes, with regard to influencing the publishing industry, "It takes four or five years, from conception through writing, editing, field testing, and publishing, to prepare a new textbook for market ... [and] when textbook buyers talk, textbook publishers listen. It is up to the reform movement to make sure the message they hear is focused on excellence."[23]

Honig's particular concern was with the dumbing down of textbooks. The term "dumbing down" was used in 1984 in a speech by the then secretary of education, Terrel Bell. The term was part of the conservative political attack on what was considered the poor quality of schools in the 1980s. By dumbing down, Honig meant lowered reading levels in texts and the lack of a point of view. He cited three causes for the dumbing down of texts. The first was the application of readability formulas to gauge the difficulty of texts. This, Honig believed, resulted in choppy and uninteresting sentences, limited vocabulary, and a trivialized content. The second cause, which was a favorite complaint by conservatives, was the overreaction by the publishing world to criticisms by women and minority groups to the existence of stereotypes in textbooks and the lack of relevant role models. Finally, Honig blamed the textbook market itself because easy textbooks full of visuals and graphics sell better than difficult textbooks.[24]

The actual process of textbook selection in California has been described in a case study by a former member of the California State Board of Education, Michael Kirst, in his book *Who Controls Our Schools?* Kirst was on the state board with Honig and shares many of his views about the quality of textbooks. According to Kirst, the state board establishes a sixteen-member advisory commission to analyze the quality of textbooks. Of the sixteen-member commission, there are generally two subject matter specialists for each field of study. In Kirst's words, these subject matter specialists, "More often than not ... decide what students should learn in the limited time available and determine the best techniques for conveying that body of knowledge." This gives these advisers a great deal of power in determining the method and content of instruction in California schools.[25]

As Kirst describes the situation during his tenure on the state board, board members did not know who the experts were in each subject matter field and had to rely on word-of-mouth recommendations. Once hired, subject matter specialists did not focus on the content of prospective textbooks, but on their appearance, methodology, and print size. In addition, the specialists were forced into tight schedules of review, while holding other full-time jobs. This resulted in specialists performing what Kirst calls the "eight-second thumb test." They would just skim the books for appearance. Kirst reports similar situations in other states where textbook reviewers are forced to make quick decisions about a large number of books. Kirst reports that in 1984 a member of the North Carolina State Board had only six weeks in which to review 700 books for one subject area.[26]

Kirst argues that dumbing down was caused by the publishers' response to the political agenda of the 1970s. Kirst writes, "The state board's agenda from 1974 to 1979 had been dominated by concerns about the bottom third of the achievement band—the disadvantaged, handicapped, or limited-English-speaking pupils." As a result, he states, "publishers had responded to market demand; they were not the cause of the problems."[27]

After his election as state superintendent of public instruction in 1982, Bill Honig changed the political agenda being used to select textbooks. The new agenda was for excellence, with an emphasis on improving the content and sharpening the point of view in textbooks. As a result of this changed political agenda, California in 1985 rejected many seventh- and eighth-grade science textbooks because they lacked strong sections on evolution, human reproduction, and other controversial topics. In 1986, California rejected K-8 mathematics books because they did not meet new curriculum guidelines.[28]

Arthur Woodward, former chair of the American Educational Research Association's special-interest group on textbooks, textbook publishing, and schools, argues that California's rejections of textbooks resulted in only superficial changes by publishers. One or two paragraphs were added to books to comply with state demands. Woodward argues that the economic structure of the publishing industry determines textbook content and not the political actions of one state. He writes, "In any event, for all the influence of California and Texas, textbooks are basically consensus documents that will sell as well in Peoria as in San Diego."[29]

While political decisions by an individual state might not affect textbooks geared for a national market, they do raise an important question about the legitimacy of state power in determining the content of textbooks. Whether or not one agrees with Honig's criticisms, should not obscure the fact that this was an attempt to apply direct political pressure to shape the content of public-school textbooks. Certainly, it is easy for many citizens to agree with Honig that school textbooks have been dumbed down and are boring to read. On the other hand, the application of direct political pressure to rectify the situation leaves the door open for the next political administration to shape textbooks in another direction. In other words, the attempted cure might just strengthen the political power that caused the problem in the first place.

In summary, the structure of the publishing industry, the existence of a national textbook market, the activities of political groups concerned with the content of textbooks, and the power of statewide adoptions results in textbooks that avoid controversy and present knowledge as neutral and official. Ultimately, students do not learn to think critically about the material presented to them in class and do not understand the controversial issues in each field of study.

THE TESTING INDUSTRY

Operating with the primary motive of profit making, the testing industry has a direct effect on students' feelings of self-worth, administrators' and teachers' ratings, students' access to college, professionals' entrance into many fields, and the content of instruction in many elementary and secondary schools. Testing, like textbook publishing, is a big business. Pick up any educational journal and you will find advertisements touting the value of particular tests. For instance, in keeping with the political emphasis on educational excellence in the mid-1980s, an advertisement by the textbook publisher Harcourt Brace Jovanich for its Metropolitan Achievement Test claims, "The new era of excellence calls for more rigorous tests. The top 23 percent is the target, with programs for excellence, higher-order thinking skills, and mastery tests." [30]

Like the textbook industry, the testing industry is concentrated among eight major firms. Some of these firms are also textbook publishers. For instance, Harcourt Brace Jovanich's testing subsidiary is the Psychological Corporation, which publishes the Metropolitan Achievement Test, Stanford Achievement Test, Wechsler Intelligence Scale, and Metropolitan Readiness Test, along with nearly 100 other titles. Houghton Mifflin, one of the top seven textbook publishers, markets thity-five major tests; and McGraw-Hill owns the California Test Bureau.

The two largest firms in the testing industry, Educational Testing Services (ETS) and American College Testing Program (ACT), are nonprofit organizations. This does not mean that they do not make a profit. They are nonprofit according to the U.S. Internal Revenue Code because they pay no money to stockholders and reinvest income into their companies. In fact, ETS, with worldwide sales in the late 1970s of $94 million, makes a 22 percent profit on tests like the Scholastic Aptitude Test (SAT).[31]

It is important to understand that the testing industry did not expand after World War II because of improved test construction. The expanded marketing of standardized tests was primarily a result of advances in production, computerized test scoring, and political and institutional demands for more testing. Oscar K. Buros, the dean of American psychometricians, and founder and editor of the *Mental Measurement Yearbook*, admitted to a gathering of his colleagues in 1977 that there had been few advances in standardized testing. He told the group, "We don't have a great deal to show for fifty years of work. ... The improvements—except for the revolutionary electronic scoring machines and computers—have not been of enough consequence to permit us to have pride in what we have accomplished. ... In fact, some of today's tests may even be poorer [than those in 1927]. ... "[32]

Changes in the testing industry have been compared to changes in the automobile industry. The real changes have taken place in marketing and production and not in the basic product. The changes in production can be seen in the history of ETS. Since its founding in 1949, ETS has steadily improved its ability to process tests by increasing automation and improving paper-processing techniques. These developments allowed ETS to reduce the percentage of workers devoted to test development and processing, and increase the number of workers involved in management and marketing. In 1949, 80 percent of the work force at ETS were professionals. By 1972, only half the work force were professionals. Only approximately 4 percent of the professional staff are involved in reviewing and writing tests. This means that more than 40 percent of the staff at ETS devote their time to managing and marketing tests. This management and promotional staff includes public relations experts, program directors, writers of corporate literature, and field representatives.[33]

Clearly, the expansion of the testing industry is the result of improved production methods and the creation of new markets. Companies like ETS devote a great deal of energy to expanding and creating new markets for their tests. The classic case of marketing occurred in the early 1970s, when ETS was forced to defend in court the National Teachers' Examination (NTE) against charges of racial discrimination. Although the court opinions were mixed regarding the extent of racial discrimination in the tests, the bad publicity caused a steady decline in the use of the NTE between 1971 and 1972. In addition to the court cases, the image of the examination was tarnished by reports that there was no significant relationship between scores on the test and teacher effectiveness.[34]

In response to the decline in sales, NTE's program director, George Elford, issued an internal memo on promotional efforts for the NTE in which he admitted that a major problem in selling the tests was the "lack of data showing test validity in predicting job performance." The memo declared that, "It does seem essential that for NTE to maintain its present net income level, promotional efforts should be directed at increasing the percentage of the teacher graduates taking the NTE." Because of the teacher surplus in the early 1970s, the memo went on to suggest that "This promotional effort should first of all be directed at school district offices, taking into account the shift from a 'seller's' market to a 'buyer's' market in teacher selection which especially affects suburban districts."[35]

Elford used three major methods for marketing the NTE. The first was to promote the NTE in scholarly publications and meetings. The second was to do a more careful analysis of the market. And lastly, ETS brought officials from institutions that might require the tests to its corporate headquarters in New Jersey and provided them with free housing and entertainment at its special conference center.[36]

Certainly, a free trip to ETS would impress any public-school official. The corporation is spread out among buildings carefully located on the 400-acre grounds of what was formerly the Stony Brook Hunt Club. The grounds, which include a putting green, tennis courts, jogging trails, picnic areas, are carefully maintained to attract songbirds, waterfowl, and deer. The conference center, which was furnished by designer Edith Queller of New York City and includes a library, sauna, and swimming pool, was managed in the 1970s by hotelier William Shearn, formerly of the Waldorf Astoria's Marco Polo Club, Laurence Rockefeller's Caneel Bay Plantation, and New York's Hotel Pierre. These surroundings probably favorably impressed many school administrators who were considering requiring the examination.[37]

The expansion of testing markets continually raises the question of how the content of tests affects the content of instruction in institutions that require or use particular tests. For example, the author of this book was directly involved in an effort to lobby ETS for the inclusion of certain types of questions on the NTE. I am a member of the American Educational Studies Association (AESA), which for many years was concerned with the lack of questions about social foundations on the NTE. A major part of the concern was purely economic. With more and more states and school districts requiring standardized examinations for teachers, the exclusion of questions on social foundations could directly affect the profession. Since it appeared that colleges of education would increasingly teach to the test, there was the possibility that fewer social foundations courses would be required of teacher candidates. Of course, fewer required courses would mean fewer jobs available for my profession.

As representatives of AESA, Professor Peter Sola of Howard University and myself went to ETS on January 3, 1986, at the invitation of Catherine Havrilesky of the NTE staff. We were entertained by the NTE staff in ETS's opulent conference center. We were informed at the meeting by Catherine Havrilesky that all projects at ETS had to show a profit within three years. We were also informed that our lobbying effort was of little value because the major political power over the content of the NTE was held by the two teachers' unions. It was, after all, the two unions that had the most power and greatest opportunity to drag ETS into court over the use of the examination.

As was mentioned previously, there is no agreed-upon standard of knowledge in any academic field—an issue that most test companies try to avoid. A good example of this occurred in 1972, when ETS released the questions on the multiple-choice Multistate Bar Exam that had been administered to aspiring lawyers in nineteen states. The faculties of two bar review courses in Washington, D.C., reviewed the test and differed on answers to 27 percent of the questions. Four other bar review faculties examined the test and differed on 35 percent of the answers. In other words, over one-third of the answers on the examination were in dispute.[38]

Besides their effect on the content of instruction, tests often place unmeasurable psychological burdens on their users. Because they are used as instruments for measuring and classifying in schools, and for screening for admission to colleges, graduate schools, professional schools, and occupations, tests contribute to a student's sense of self-worth. Allan Nairn and his associates provide a case study of Gary Valdik, who, although he was in the top tenth of his high school class, received a low score on his SAT. As Valdik told the story, students who received low SAT scores at his school tended to lie to their classmates about their test results, while those who scored high were bathed in glory. The students, of course, believed that their SAT test scores were an accurate measure of their academic worth—and, in many cases, their social worth. Gary believed his score was accurate because, in his words, "it's a standardized test. It was stripping us of everything and measuring us as equals."[39]

Gary claimed that it took him four years to recover from the psychological effects of his low SAT scores. He did not seek psychological help because he assumed that it was a valid test. The agricultural school he wanted to attend told him that his school record and outside accomplishments were impressive, but his SAT scores were too low for admission. He attended a smaller college and achieved a high grade point average. Eventually, he was able to enter and succeed in the agricultural school that had first rejected him on the basis of his SAT scores. Even after fighting a battle with hepatitis, Gary was able to maintain a 3.3 grade point average on a 4-point scale. Certainly, similar stories could be told of elementary and high school students whose sense of self-worth was lowered by scores on standardized tests.

CONCLUSION

Profit is the major interest of the publishing and testing industries. The fact that the market in both industries is concentrated in the hands of a few firms reduces innovation and risk taking. In addition, political forces shape the products of both industries. Publishers fear controversy and test makers fear being taken to court. For publishers, the possibility of harmful controversy hurting profits results in textbooks noted for their blandness and lack of a point of view. For test makers, the fear of going to court usually results in tests that please those who threaten court action.

At this point in time, it is not clear how successful states like California will be in pressuring publishers to change textbooks. Even if successful, it raises a host of questions about how legitimate it is for state governments to determine the content of textbooks. After all, Bill Honig and other elected and educational politicians have a particular political point of view regarding what knowledge is of most worth. It is certainly questionable whether or not their points of view should be imposed on school textbooks. Even if one accepts the idea that politicians should determine the content of textbooks, then there is the question of what happens when a new set of politicians with different ideas is elected to office. Do textbooks then change with each change in political administration?

Of considerable interest for the future is the trend for publishing houses to operate testing subsidiaries. Obviously, a company can now publish a textbook and a standardized test that are parallel in method and content. What with state governments working together to influence textbook publishing, under these combined political pressures and economic interests, knowledge could become standardized across the entire nation.

SOME INTERIM CONSIDERATIONS

It is worthwhile to pause at this stage and consider the political structure of education in the United States as described in the previous four chapters. It is certainly legitimate now to wonder whether the costs of the current structure are worth the price of progress that may be made and whether progress actually occurs. One method of evaluating the political sytem is to consider the actual process of bringing about educational change. Let us imagine how an individual might bring about a change in the overall goals of American education.

First, the individual would dismiss the idea of beginning at the level of the local school district. At this time, local educational politics is marginal politics. Local school politics involves a process of adapting state and federal educational policies to the social and economic needs of local communities. In other words, working for change in local school systems is the final step in bringing about changes in educational policies at the national level.

In the 1970s and 1980s, the real power in education lies at the state and federal levels. As discussed in Chapter 4, individual legislators are the most influential educational policy makers in state governments. The strongest influences on state educational policies outside of government are the business community and the teachers' unions. Therefore, political work at the state level begins with convincing teachers' unions and the business community that the proposed changes are in their interests. For instance, in some states during the 1980s school reformers promised teachers an improved profession and business an improved economy.

After the teachers unions' and business groups have agreed to support the proposed educational changes, they should then bring pressure to bear on state legislators who specialize in educational issues. Maximum pressure can be applied if the proposed changes are turned into a single-issue campaign.

Aid should also be solicited from the state educational bureaucracy. The key is winning the support of the chief state school officer. In states such as California, where the chief state school officer is elected, business groups and teachers' unions can offer campaign support in exchange for the candidate's support of the proposed educational changes. In other words, at the state level the support of business groups and teachers' unions is essential for making major changes in educational policies.

At the federal level, planning a strategy for educational change is more difficult because of the role of national political parties. The first thing an individual must do is choose a national political party. This choice depends on the nature of the proposed educational changes and how they would be accepted by the educational constituency of each party. In the mid-1980s, promises to restore traditional values in public schools, improve the economy and national defense, and supply aid to private schools would win the support of the educational constituency of the Republican Party. On the other hand, educational proposals that would promote the interests of the teachers' unions, promise aid to ethnic and minority groups, and bolster the national economy would be supported by the educational constituency of the Democratic Party.

If the party that supports the proposed educational changes gains control of the executive and congressional branches, then an individual would work to gain passage of legislation that provided appropriate categorical grants. With categorical grants, state and local school systems would implement that proposed educational changes in order to receive federal funds.

Implementation of the legislation, as discussed in Chapter 3, would create new state and local bureaucratic structures. The administrators in the new bureaucracy would form an interest group to protect and expand the legislation. In addition, iron triangles would form between politicians, the new administrative positions, and interest groups outside of government.

To provide a knowledge base, federal money would be appropriated to fund educational research into issues related to the educational changes. Always in need of new sources of funding, educational researchers would write research proposals regarding such changes. These educational researchers would report their findings at national meetings and form a research interest group. This new interest group would lobby the government for more research funding in this new area.

To ensure continued federal support, educational researchers would develop an elaborate intellectual justification for the importance of their work. Convinced of the value of their efforts, these researchers would campaign to make their area of study a central focus of teacher training. Consequently, the fruits of their research would join the tangled web of subject matter in teacher education.

Obviously, all of these endeavors will eventually have an effect on local school systems. As discussed in Chapter 5, the actual form the new legislation and research findings would take in the schools would be a function of local economies, power structures, educational bureaucracies, and the local teachers' unions. Given the variations between communities, one never knows what factor will have the greatest impact.

It is quite conceivable that by the time these changes begin to affect local schools, the original problem that prompted the educational reform would have ended or the political leadership would have changed. It is also possible that a new set of social and economic concerns would have created a new reform agenda. While the educational system is adjusting to these new priorities, students would be educated in a curriculum shaped for problems that no longer exist.

In fact, because of the slowness of change, what students actually study might always be out of sync with outside realities. For instance, one wonders how many students studying cosmetology, auto body repair, and other subjects in vocational schools in the 1970s were able to get jobs in their field. If such students are unable to find jobs in these fields, then the actual cost of education would have to include the time wasted by students in obsolete vocational courses. It is difficult, after considering the above scenario, to justify the costs and outcomes of the current political structure of American education. It is hopelessly entangled in conflicting interest groups, administrative levels, and the actions of elected and educational politicians. At times this complex political structure pursues a continually shifting vision of what will benefit schoolchildren, while at other times it is driven by simple greed.

NOTES

1. *Transcript of Proceedings before the Commissioner of Education and the State Textbook Committee, July 14–16, 1986* (Austin, Tex.: Kennedy Reporting Service, 1986), p. 182.
2. Ibid., p. 183.
3. Ibid., p. 29.
4. Ibid., p. 31.
5. Ibid., p. 169.
6. Ibid., pp. 243–44.
7. "The Ruling in *Mozert v. Hawkins County Public Schools,*" *Education Week*, Vol. 6, No. 9 (November 5, 1986), 18.
8. For a discussion of this case and other issues involving academic freedom, see Joel Spring, *American Education: An Introduction to Social and Political Aspects*, 3rd ed. (White Plains, N.Y.: Longman, 1985), pp. 248–57.
9. Robert Rothman, "Wall Street 'Frenzy' Aiding Consolidation of Textbook Industry," *Education Week*, Volume 6, No. 9 (November 5, 1986), 1.
10. Ibid., pp. 1, 21.
11. Ibid., p. 21.
12. Lewis A. Coser, Charles Kadushin, and Walter W. Powell, *Books: The Culture and Commerce of Publishing* (Chicago: University of Chicago Press, 1982), pp. 23–24.
13. Ibid., p. 24.
14. These observations are the result of my own investigation of the college

textbook industry in 1986. I observed the process of decision making regarding textbooks, and the interactions of editors and authors as described in the following paragraph.

15. Coser et al., *Books*, pp. 71–92, 200–24.
16. Frances Fitzgerald, *America Revised: History Schoolbooks in the Twentieth Century* (Boston: Little, Brown, 1979), p. 37.
17. Harold Rugg, "Do the Social Studies Prepare Pupils Adequately for Life Activities?" in Guy Whipple, ed., *The Twenty-Second Yearbook of the National Society for the Study of Education Part II: The Social Studies in the Elementary and Secondary School* (Bloomington: Public School Publishing House, 1973), pp. 1–27.
18. Fitzgerald, *America Revised*, p. 175.
19. Ibid., p. 37.
20. Dean Jaros, *Socialization to Politics* (New York: Praeger, 1973), p. 105.
21. *Transcript of Proceedings*, pp. 18–19.
22. Bill Honig, *Last Chance for Our Children: How You Can Help Save Our Schools* (Reading, Mass.: Addison-Wesley, 1985), p. 135.
23. Ibid., p. 135.
24. Ibid., pp. 130–32.
25. Michael W. Kirst, *Who Controls Our Schools?—American Values in Conflict* (New York: W. H. Freeman, 1984), pp. 115–16.
26. Ibid., pp. 116–18.
27. Ibid., p. 120.
28. Arthur Woodward, "On Teaching and Textbook Publishing: Political Issues Obscure Questions of Pedagogy," *Education Week*, Vol. 6, No. 17 (January 21, 1987), 28.
29. Ibid., p. 22.
30. Advertisement in *Phi Delta Kappan*, Vol. 68, No. 4 (November 1986), 265.
31. Allan Nairn and associates, *The Reign of ETS: The Corporation That Makes Up Minds* (Washington, D.C.: Ralph Nader Report on the Educational Testing Service, 1980), pp. 40–41, 299, 337.
32. Quoted in ibid., p. 315.
33. Ibid., pp. 315–16.
34. Ibid., pp. 319–20.
35. Quoted in ibid., p. 321.
36. Ibid., p. 322.
37. Ibid., pp. 36–38.
38. Ibid., p. 140.
39. Quoted in ibid., p. 7.

CHAPTER 7

The Political Uses of Courts

In this chapter we shall analyze the political uses of the judicial system rather than supply a broad review of all the court decisions that have affected the public schools. Of particular importance are class action suits brought against school districts by religious, racial, language, and handicapped minorities seeking protection under the First and Fourteenth amendments to the Constitution.

Minority groups have often turned to the court system because they lack the political power to receive redress for their grievances through the application of pressure on school boards, state legislatures, and the federal government. For instance, minority religious groups like the Amish have had to protect their religion against majority political power by turning to the courts.[1] Black populations in the South, because of voter discrimination, have not been able to achieve integrated education through the usual political process; they too were forced to turn to the court system.[2] Lacking political power, handicapped and minority language groups have also used the courts to achieve political ends.[3]

The use of the courts to achieve political goals raises several important issues. One is the problem of representation in a class action suit. Is the group bringing a class action suit truly representative of the population it claims to represent? Consider the situation in the 1986 case, *Smith v. Board of School Commissioners of Mobile County*, in which a group of 600 Mobile, Alabama, residents charged the local public schools with violating the First Amendment to the Constitution by teaching secular humanism. U.S. District Judge W. Brevard Hand certified the case, based on the actions of these 600 Mobile residents, as being a class action suit brought by all Alabama parents and citizens who believe in God.[4] Obviously, it would be impossible to determine if this group of citizens actually represented the views of all those believing in God in Alabama. In fact, the judge's decision to make it a class action suit implied that the defenders and their lawyers did not believe in God.

The Alabama case highlights many of the problems in class action suits. Not only is there a problem of determining whether or not a group truly represents a particular class of people, but also whether or not they represent all the divergent views among a class of people. For instance, probably not all people in the state of Alabama who believe in God think that the schools teach secular humanism, nor do they believe that the content of public schooling should be changed. Consider the same situation with regard to school desegregation cases. Members of the black community have differed sharply over court remedies. Some have favored busing, while others have argued for community control and alternative schools. In these cases, which remedies truly represent the views of the black community?

In response to the issue of representation in class action suits, it can be argued that while courts initially deal with parochial interests, their final decisions have broad social implications and involve basic constitutional issues. In addition, while it is impossible for the courts to canvass diverse viewpoints in a class action suit, they can rely on the evidence given in the actual litigation. But even with these considerations, representation in a class action suit remains a problem.[5]

There is also an issue regarding the court's ability to deal with the evidence presented in education cases. Much of this evidence involves test scores, educational statistics, and research findings. Very seldom is this material presented without dispute. For instance, in the case of standardized tests, not only can the tests themselves be disputed but also the meaning of their results. The same is true of statistics and research findings. There is very little in the world of education that can be presented as undisputed fact.

Consequently, judges must rule on evidence that is presented in a form outside their normal training and that is contested by educational practitioners. Historically, the courts have relied on cross-examination to establish specific facts. In court cases involving social science evidence, judges must rely on the cross-examination of expert witnesses. In evaluating social science evidence, judges have to determine which expert witness is correct. Certainly, the ability of judges to choose between social science experts and understand social science information can be questioned.[6]

A similar issue arises when courts specify remedies in their decisions. It is difficult for a judge to know the possible educational and social consequences of certain remedies. Sometimes, at least according to critics of school desegregation decisions, court decrees have had a serious negative effect on the problems in need of correction. Critics also claim that in many circumstances judges are unable to enforce their decrees.[7]

All of these issues are directly related to the use of the courts by political groups to achieve changes in educational policies. The problems of representation in class action suits, the ability of the court to judge educational evidence, and the ability to implement complex remedies have to be considered in analyzing educational policies that are the result of court action.

Of course, the most important issue is the protection of constitutional rights. While one might criticize the political use of the courts, one must always remember that protection of constitutional rights is an important part of the political system in the United States.

This chapter will discuss the political uses of the courts by briefly describing the major constitutional issues that affect education and by analyzing the methods used in particular class action court cases.

CONSTITUTIONAL ISSUES

The First and Fourteenth amendments to the Constitution are the focus of most class action suits in education. One major exception is the Eighth Amendment, which prohibits "cruel and unusual punishment." The Eighth Amendment has been an issue in suits brought against public schools for practicing corporal punishment. In the most important of these suits, *Ingraham v. Wright* (1977), the U.S. Supreme Court ruled that corporal punishment was not "cruel and unusual," because it had been a traditional method of maintaining discipline in public schools, and that although public opinion was divided on the issue, there did not seem to be any trend toward eliminating its use.[8]

The First Amendment is appealed to in suits involving religion and free speech. Often both sides in religious disputes rely on the First Amendment because it both protects the free exercise of religion and prohibits the government from supporting religion. For instance, those opposed to organized prayer in public schools argue that it is banned by the First Amendment, while supporters argue that the free-exercise requirement of the First Amendment protects school prayer. In recent years, Protestant fundamentalists have invoked the First Amendment in charges that the public schools teach secular humanism.

The First Amendment states:

Congress shall make no law respecting an establishment of religion, or prohibiting the free exercise thereof; or abridging the freedom of speech, or of the press; or the right of the people peaceably to assemble, and to petition the Government for a redress of grievances.

Religious minorities have sought protection from the public schools' interfering with their religious practices by invoking the prohibition against government interference with the free exercise of religion. For instance, in the 1940s the Jehovah's Witnesses success-fully argued before the Supreme Court that the public schools' requirement to say the Pledge of Allegiance interfered with their practice of religion because they believed that the obligations imposed by the laws of God were superior to the laws of government. One of the laws of God taken literally by Jehovah's Witnesses is, "Thou shall not make unto thee any graven image, or any likeness of anything that is in heaven above, or that is in the earth beneath, or that is in the water under the earth; thus shalt not bow down thyself to them nor serve them." Jehovah's Witnesses believe that the flag is an image and refuse, for religious reasons, to salute it. In this particular case, the Supreme Court agreed that the Pledge of Allegiance requirement did interfere with the free exercise of religion.[9]

One of the classic cases in which a religious minority desired protection of its beliefs against the public schools is *State of Wisconsin, Petitioner v. Jona Yoder et al.* This case involved a group of Amish who, as a political and religious minority, had continually felt threatened by compulsory education laws. As a political minority, there was little they could do to change state and local laws regarding education. As a religious minority, they found that the public schools were teaching values contrary to their religious beliefs. For instance, one objection of Amish parents to compulsory high school attendance was the require-ment that girls wear shorts for physical education, which is a serious violation of Amish beliefs. The Amish also objected to the public high school's broad curriculum and its vocational and college preparatory courses. (The Amish do their own vocational training within their communities.) In addition, the Amish objected to an education that stresses critical thinking and asking questions.[10]

Unable to achieve their goals through normal political channels, the Amish community in New Glarus, Wisconsin, went to court in 1968 to fight state compulsory education laws. School authorities argued that compulsory education laws were necessary to protect the general welfare of the state, while the Amish argued that such laws were a violation of their free exercise of religion. The Supreme Court ruled in favor of the Amish, arguing that "We can accept it as settled, therefore, that however strong the State's interest in universal compulsory education, it is by no means absolute to the exclusion or subordination of all other interests." [11]

The First Amendment prohibition against the establishment of religion has been invoked by groups seeking to change religious practices in the public schools or the values being taught. Again, the courts have been used to cause changes in educational policies. The classic case is the school prayer decision in *Engel v. Vitale* (1962). In this case, the New York Board of Regents granted a local school district the right to have a brief prayer in each class at the beginning of the school day. The prayer was voluntary and considered denominationally neutral. The prayer stated, "Almighty God, we acknowledge our dependence upon Thee, and we beg Thy blessings upon us, our parents, our teachers, and our country." The Supreme Court ruled that this was a clear violation of the First Amendment prohibition against the establishment of religion because a government official had written the prayer. The Court stated that "in this country it is not part of the business of government to compose official prayers for any group of the American people to recite as a part of the religious program carried on by government." [12]

In addition, as mentioned in the case involving a class action suit by all citizens of Alabama believing in God, groups have invoked the First Amendment in their claims that the schools teach secular humanism. These arguments provided a new twist to the concept of the establishment of religion. Carried to the extreme, it could mean any teaching of values could be construed as the teaching of religion. The obvious difficulty in these arguments is linking the teaching of values such as secular humanism to an established religion.

The Free-Speech Clause of the First Amendment has been used to protect student rights. In the most famous case, *Tinker v. Des Moines Independent School District* (1969), a group of students was suspended from school for wearing armbands in protest against the Vietnam War. The Supreme Court, ruling in favor of the students, stated that a student "may express his opinion, even on controversial subjects like the conflict in Vietnam. . . . Under our Constitution, free speech is not a right that is given only to be so circumscribed that it exists in principle but not in fact." [13]

Minority religious and language groups have used the Fourteenth Amendment to pressure schools for equality of educational opportunity. In addition, the Fourteenth Amendment has been used to protect due process rights. The Fourteenth Amendment states:

> All persons born or naturalized in the United States, and subject to the jurisdiction thereof, are citizens of the United States and of the State wherein they reside. No State shall make or enforce any law which shall abridge the privileges or immunities of citizens of the United States; nor shall any State deprive any person of life, liberty, or property without due process of law; nor deny to any person within its jurisdiction the equal protection of the laws.

The clause in the amendment stating "nor shall any State deprive any person of life, liberty, or property without due process of law" has been used to protect a student's right to an education and a teacher's right to employment. The courts consider state provision of schooling and the employment of teachers to be a property right that cannot be taken away without due process. So, for instance, in *Goss v. Lopez* (1975), the Supreme Court argued that suspension from school involved a property right. The Court ruled that due process "requires, in connection with a suspension of 10 days or less, that the student be given oral or written notice of the charges against him and, if he denies them, an explanation of the evidence the authorities have and an opportunity to present his side of the story." The Court based its decision on "legitimate claims of entitlement to public education" as given in state law.[14]

Politically, the most important part of the Fourteenth Amendment is the Equal-Protection Clause, which states: "nor deny to any person within its jurisdiction the equal protection of the laws." Under the Equal-Protection Clause, if any state government provides a system of education, then it must be provided equally to all people in the state. Certainly, one of the most fundamental revolutionary concepts of the eighteenth and nineteenth centuries was the idea that all people must be equally treated by the law.

With regard to education, the concept of equal treatment has proved to be extremely complex. Consider the issue of segregation. The Supreme Court ruled in the nineteenth century that school segregation was constitutional as long as equal facilities and instruction were provided. In 1954, the Supreme Court reversed the ruling by arguing that segregated schools were inherently unequal and, therefore, violated the Equal-Protection Clause of the Fourteenth Amendment.[15]

In another example, consider the issue of language. Does the fact that a child does not speak English deny him or her an equal opportunity to gain the advantages of a state-provided education? The Supreme Court answered Yes to the question in *Lau et al. v. Nichols et al.* (1974). The case was a class action suit brought in behalf of non-English-speaking Chinese students in the San Francisco School District. The complaint was that no special instruction for learning standard English had been provided to these students. The Supreme Court ruled that special aid had to be given to students for whom English was not a standard language; otherwise, the school system was not providing equal educational opportunity. The Court based this ruling on Title VI of the 1964 Civil Rights Act, which bans discrimination based on "race, color, or national origin."[16]

In general, the concept of the state providing equal educational opportunity has been used to question educational practices ranging from tracking to school finance. Any practice that appears to exclude an identifiable group of children from equal participation in education is open to question in the courts. In some situations, like school finance cases, actions are limited to state courts. In *Rodriguez v. San Antonio Independent School District* (1978), the Supreme Court ruled against the plaintiffs, who were arguing that unequal educational funding was in violation of the Fourteenth Amendment. In its decision, the Court stated, "The consideration and initiation of fundamental reforms with respect to state taxation and education are matters reserved for the legislative processes of the various states."[17] This meant that school finance issues related to equal protection would have to be decided on a state-by-state basis within state court systems.

In summary, while a wide range of legal issues exists in education, the First and the Fourteenth amendments of the Constitution have been the primary concern of groups using the courts to achieve changes in educational policies. As mentioned in the introduction to the chapter, these types of court cases require an analysis of the representativeness of the plaintiffs in class action suits, an analysis of the ability of the courts to understand testimony based on educational research and statistics, and the ability of the courts to determine remedies.

THE *OTERO* CASE

Otero v. Mesa County Valley School District No. 51 is one of the case studies used by Michael Rebell and Arthur Block in their national study of the effects of courts on educational policy making.[18] This case provides an example of the problems of representativeness of plaintiffs and the capabilities of the courts. It is one of the four major case studies Rebell and Block use to explore the general debate about the role of the courts in determining social policy. In addition to the four case studies, they analyze sixty-five federal court proceedings that deal with educational isues.

The overall goal of Rebell and Block's study is to determine the legitimacy of judicial action on social policy issues. As for representativeness, in 71 percent of the cases, the plaintiffs requested class action status. In 36 percent of the cases, the court ignored or neglected to determine whether or not the group was truly representative of the class it claimed to represent. "Thus," Rebell and Block write, "although plaintiffs purport to speak for broad classes, available judicial mechanisms for verifying claims of representativeness are not applied with regularity." [19]

In analyzing the ability of courts to deal with evidence from the social sciences, Rebell and Block found that most judges avoid basing judicial decisions on social science evidence. In their study, judges did not decide complex social issues, even though social science facts were introduced in forty-two of the sixty-five cases. In half of these situations, judges based their decisions on legal issues, not on social science evidence. Rebell and Block found, however, that most judges had a reasonable working knowledge of social science concepts and language.

Rebell and Block found in thirteen of the fifteen cases in which the judge had ordered a remedy that involved major reform of an educational system, defendants and public agencies had played a major role in drafting the court decree. This participation involved the basic drafting of orders and the negotiation of details. In only one of these fifteen cases had the judge assumed sole responsibility for drafting the court order.

In general, Rebell and Block found that the courts' involvement in social issues has created a political role that had not been considered in the traditional judicial system. Of particular importance is the fact that the courts' method of political involvement is quite different from that of a legislative body. For instance, judges use an analytical fact-finding method that depends on the weighing of evidence from experts. On the other hand, political decisions in legislative organizations are achieved through compromise and accommodation by various interest groups. In other words, judges reason about evidence while politicians strike bargains.

In this political role, Rebell and Block were favorably impressed by the ability of judges to gather and evaluate social science evidence, and deal with diverse interest groups in class action suits. Consequently, they do not believe that the real issue is whether or not courts are capable of dealing with social problems. What they see as the real issue is whether or not a given political decision should be made by a judge or by legislators.

Formulating the issue in this manner leads to a different set of considerations. On the one hand, judges can be considered to be rational decision makers who decide on the basis of an analytical judicial process. On the other hand, elected political officials can be viewed as decision makers who depend on bargaining and compromise. Within this framework, the question becomes "whether particular aspects of social problems should be handled through the principled, analytical judicial process or through the instrumental, mutual adjustment patterns of the legislatures."[20]

Given this orientation, Rebell and Block use the *Otero* case study to illustrate the problems faced by the judiciary when dealing with social issues. The case highlights the problems of the representativeness of plaintiffs and the capabilities of courts to deal with social science evidence.

When the *Otero* case was initiated in 1974 by lawyers from the Mexican American Legal Defense Fund (MALDEF), the Chicano Education Project (CEP), and the Colorado Rural Legal Assistance (CRLA), there was an immediate conflict over the issue of representation. Based on an analysis of test scores and personnel records, the plaintiffs accused the local school district of not providing equal educational opportunity for Chicano children and demanded bilingual education services. The local school board expressed its strong hostility to the legal action because it believed it represented the interests and needs of local Chicano children, and that the plaintiffs were primarily outside agitators. Not only did the school board dismiss most of the plaintiffs as not representative of the local Chicano community, but it also accused one local Chicano leader of using the case to advance his political fortunes.

In certifying the case as a class action suit, district judge Fred Winner ignored arguments given by the defense that none of the plaintiffs was deficient in English and that some had achieved high levels of education. Indeed, at the beginning of the case, there was little support for the suit in the local Chicano community. But the fact that it was declared a class action suit made it possible for the plaintiffs to present the case as a crusade on behalf of the entire local Chicano community. As part of the crusade, the plaintiffs believed that one of their goals was educating the local community to the educational problems in the local school system.

Therefore, as the case began, the whole issue of representation was thrown open to question by the public. While the court recognized it as a class action, the public debated how well the plaintiffs represented the local Chicano community.

The major legal issue in the case forced the court to deal with social science evidence. The focus was on the Supreme Court decision in *Lau v. Nichols*. The plaintiffs wanted to prove that Anglo children in the school district substantially outperformed Chicano children, and that bilingual education services therefore needed to be established. On the other side, the defendants (the local school board) argued that it had met the requirements of the *Lau* decision by providing transitional English instruction for students with language problems.

Specifically, the plaintiffs claimed that all Chicano children were discriminated against by an Anglo-oriented curriculum. The curriculum, the plaintiffs argued, resulted in lower academic achievement scores. To achieve equal educational opportunity, it was argued, the local school district would be required to consider cultural differences in the planning of educational programs. Given this legal argument, the plaintiffs needed to establish in court that Chicano students did have lower academic achievement scores as compared to Anglos, and that the differences in test scores were the result of cultural bias in the curriculum.

In deciding the case, Judge Winner had to consider highly controversial social science evidence dealing with test validity and educational programming. The case opened with the plaintiffs claiming that 80 percent of the class they represented were proficient in Spanish, while the defendants argued that only 19 percent came from Spanish-speaking homes and that none were fluent in Spanish. The plaintiffs claimed 54 percent lacked ability in English, while the defendants claimed that only 5 percent had difficulty with English.

To support their case, the plaintiffs introduced information from three school surveys. One survey had been taken by teachers on whether or not Spanish was spoken in students' homes. The second survey had examined student records to find remarks regarding language problems. And the third survey had been done of the homes of Spanish-surnamed students to determine whether Spanish was spoken in the household. As noted by Rebell and Block, none of these surveys had dealt directly with the language proficiencies of the students.

The survey evidence was presented for the plaintiffs by an expert witness and psychologist, Dr. Steve Moreno. He claimed that it demonstrated that 80 percent of the Spanish-surnamed children had significant Spanish-language abilities.

The real debate over social science evidence was opened when the defendants introduced test data that they claimed showed that only a few Chicano children were proficient in Spanish. Consequently, the defendants argued that bilingual education was not needed but only remedial education courses. The plaintiffs countered by arguing that the test lacked content validity. In response, the defendants brought in an expert in sociolinguistics who argued that the test did have content validity. The plaintiffs then introduced an expert witness who claimed that the test was not valid in that part of Colorado because it had been standardized in El Paso, Texas, where Mexican-Americans spoke a different dialect. The plaintiffs then questioned the ability of the testers, who admitted that they were unfamiliar with the testing guidelines of the American Psychological Association. The defendants countered by claiming that the formulators of the American Psychological Association standards had an axe to grind and compared the standards to an automobile manufacturer's recommendation to use a certain brand of oil in a new car.

The problems faced by judges in dealing with social science evidence are exemplified by the testimony given by the defense's star expert witness Dr. Gene Glass, a professor of education at the University of Colorado. Glass testified that the differences in achievement test scores between Anglo and Chicano students in the school district were not a result of an Anglo-dominated curriculum. He argued that the explanation could be found in differences in intelligence (IQ test scores) and socioeconomic status.

Marshalling a whole range of social science studies, Glass maintained that all research showed that IQ and socioeconomic status were the best predictors of scores on achievement tests. Therefore, he asserted, one must control for socioeconomic status and IQ before one can determine the impact of cultural and linguistic differences. This could be done, using his methodology, by classifying students according to ethnicity, IQ, and socioeconomic status. If IQ and socioeconomic status were similar for Anglo and Chicano students, and achievement scores were different, then, Glass argued, one could ascribe the differences to cultural or linguistic causes. After grouping the school district's students by ethnicity, IQ, and socioeconomic status, Glass concluded that the differences between Anglo and Chicano students were only minor. Anglos were one month ahead of Chicano in reading and 1.8 months in language, while Chicanos were ahead of Anglos in mathematics by 3 months.

The plaintiffs attacked Glass's testimony by arguing that IQ tests are culturally and linguistically biased. Glass countered that his method compensated for bias in both the IQ and achievement tests. The only problem that could exist, Glass claimed, is if the IQ test were more biased than the achievement test. Glass also argued that IQ tests were geared to the level of language proficiency demonstrated on other tests by Chicano students in the school district.

The fact that Glass's evidence was accepted by the judge, according to Rebell and Block, is a good example of the difficulty the judiciary has with social science evidence. From their perspective, Glass's evidence was full of methodological and logical errors. They demonstrate how Glass's data could have been manipulated to show significant differences in language and reading performance between Anglos and Chicanos. In the end, the major failure was the result of the plaintiffs not adequately analyzing and responding to Glass's findings.

In this situation, the court failed to be an adequate arena for the judgment of social science data. The legal process depends on an adversarial relationship in which evidence is adequately evaluated by expert witnesses representing both sides of a case. If one side does not prepare adequately, then the whole process fails as a mechanism for dealing with research information. In the words of Rebell and Block, "What is pertinent here is that the mechanisms of adversarial presentation of social science data apparently did not, on this occasion, elicit a well-balanced perspective on the critical issues."[21]

The lawyers for the defense were given a better understanding of social science methodology than the lawyers for the plaintiffs. Glass spent many hours coaching the lawyers for the school board on social science methodology the lawyers for the plaintiffs, on the other hand, apparently had little training for cross-examination on social science issues. In addition, Glass proved to be a very good witness who was able to steer the plaintiff's lawyers away from the greatest problem in his data—namely, that Chicanos in his classification did better than Anglos in mathematics but not in language. This opened up the possibility (which was never taken by the plantiff's lawyers) of using Glass's results to prove the linguistic bias of the curriculum.

In his decision in favor of the school board, Judge Winner stated that the expert witnesses for the school board had made more sense than had the expert witnesses for the plaintiffs. In fact, Judge Winner presented his own detailed analysis of the comparative validity of the plaintiff's surveys and defendant's standardized tests. He dismissed the failure of the school district to follow the testing guidelines of the American Psychological Association as being merely a technical issue.

Otero provides a good example of the problems faced by the courts in dealing with social science evidence, and it demonstrates the problem of the representativeness of a group bringing a class action suit. It was never established that in fact the plaintiffs did represent the majority of the local Chicano population.

In addition, there is the larger issue, raised by Rebell and Block, about whether the courts, with their adversarial means of handling social science evidence are a better place for certain types of political action than are legislative bodies, which operate on compromise and accommodation.

HOBSON V. HANSEN

The case of *Hobson v. Hansen* exemplifies the difficulties faced by courts in providing remedies for social problems. It is one of the four detailed case studies used by Donald Horowitz in his book, *The Courts and Social Policy*. Horowitz is highly critical of court involvement in social policy issues. He finds that differences between the methods of legal and social science inquiry create major problems in litigation. For instance, because they rely on an adversarial relationship to gather information, the courts do not go directly to the sources when dealing with social science evidence, but rely on the hearsay evidence of expert witnesses. This situation, Horowitz argues, leaves judges at the mercy of advocates and interpreters of social science data and restricts the souces of their information. "So far," Horowitz writes, "expert witnesses have had too much latitude to parade their own preferences as science." The previously discussed *Otero* case provides evidence of this problem. Horowitz proposes, "It would be far preferable to admit books and articles on matters of social fact directly into evidence as exhibits, not require as a precondition that an expert refer to them in his testimony, abolish the favored position of government reports, and permit counsel to attack the reliability of studies directly."[22]

Courts also have difficulty handling social science data in the implementation of remedies. Very often, courts are unable to adequately predict the ultimate consequences of a judicial plan to remedy a social problem. In trying to predict the outcome of a remedy, courts must rely on predictions made by competing social science experts. The same types of problems occur in court remedies based on social science information as occur in court decisions based on social science data. In addition, Horowitz argues, courts are often limited in their ability to supervise their remedies and monitor the consequences. In Horowitz's words, "The record suggests that the courts are better equipped with machinery to discovery the past than to forecast the future."[23]

Hobson v. Hansen is Horowitz's prime example of the problems of judicial implementation.[24] The case was initiated by Julius Hobson in 1966 against the Washington, D.C., school system for denying black and poor children equal educational opportunity. Prior to the suit, the District of Columbia had, until the 1954 *Brown* decision, maintained a racially separate dual school system. In response to the requirement to end the dual school system, the school board tried to find other means of maintaining segregation. One method was to allow students to transfer from one school zone to another with lower enrollments. These transfers, it was determined in court, usually favored whites and maintained segregated schools. In addition, Superintendent Carl Hansen introduced a tracking system in 1957 that resulted in further segregation. Circuit Court Judge J. Skelley Wright identified both the transfer system and tracking plan as fostering segregation.

Of major concern to Judge Wright, and eventually the central feature of the court's plan to end inequality of educational opportunity, was the unequal distribution of financial resources in the Washington, D.C., school system. Judge Wright argued that if whites and blacks, or the rich and poor, were in separate schools, then there had to be a measurable means of maintaining equality between schools. For Judge Wright, this measurable means was financial expenditures.

In 1967, Judge Wright issued *Hobson I*, which abolished optional zones and required faculty integration and voluntary busing. The decision also abolished the established tracking system. It was assumed that expenditures among schools would equalize as a result of these actions.

In 1970, Julius Hobson again returned to court with claims that school expenditures had not been equalized. In fact, there were few positive results under the decree from *Hobson I*. Both voluntary busing and voluntary teacher transfers for integration proved ineffective. Large financial differences between schools still existed.

In *Hobson II*, Judge Wright decided to focus on the issue of unequal expenditures. The major question that had to be answered was what should be equalized. The court now entered the tricky arena of educational research to establish a link between educational expenditures and equality of educational opportunity. For instance, equal amounts of money spent on cafeterias or maintenance might not result in equal educational opportunity. In fact, at the time, more money was being spent on building new schools in black, as opposed to white, neighborhoods.

The court therefore had to go through the process of narrowing the issue of unequal expenditures. In this regard, the lawyers played an important role. Initially, the court considered a wide range of resources that could be equalized between schools, including equalization of teachers according to their measured verbal abilities, equalization of all resources, equalization of teachers according to years of experience, and equalization of pupil-teacher ratios. The final decision was to focus on per-pupil expenditures in each school. Per-pupil expenditures provided a measurable standard that could be administered by the courts.

The court further narrowed the issue of per-pupil expenditures to teachers' salaries. One option was to consider per-pupil expenditures in a school according to the total sum of money spent on textbooks, library resources, and salaries of the entire staff. The court held that there was a right to an equal per-pupil distribution of teacher services and that the best measure of this was teacher costs. The court, in its decree, did not consider teacher costs according to different components. For instance, no distinctions were made between the costs of classroom teachers and special subject teahers. Nor were teacher costs adjusted for pupil-teacher ratios.

One problem with narrowing the issue of equality to teacher costs per pupil was the lack of agreement that inequalities in this cost factor were related to race or income. Lawyers for the plaintiffs and defendants argued over whether the correlation between parent income and per-pupil costs of teachers was weakly positive or weakly negative. Like many social science disputes, the issue hinged on methodology, with one side using a rank-order correlation and the other a Pearson product-moment correlation. Reflecting the problems courts have with this type of dispute, Judge Wright dismissed the whole debate as an abstruse statistical dispute.

Judge Wright avoided the entire issue of the relationship between parent income and pre-pupil teacher costs, and focused on the wealth of the neighborhood surrounding each school. Wright also refused to accept arguments dealing with the size of the school. For instance, the plaintiff's lawyers used the testimony of an expert witness in economics to establish that the size of a school accounted for one-third of the difference in per-pupil teacher costs between schools. This economic argument raised the issue of economies of scale. In larger schools it is easier to establish optimal pupil-to-teacher ratios. In smaller elementary schools the costs of special-subject teachers in art, foreign languages, music, mathematics, physical education, reading and science are absorbed by fewer students. Therefore, the costs of teachers per-pupil tend to be higher in smaller schools.

Trying to establish the value of narrowing the remedy for inequality of educational opportunity to teacher costs per pupil increased the complexity of the court's consideration of social science data. In Horowitz's words, "Data were available on the issue of economies of scale, but important factual and legal gaps remained. Each legal question turned on the resolution of an empirical question, which then turned out to have another legal question embedded within it." From Horowitz's perspective, "The legal question of inequality depended on the empirical question of economies of scale." [25]

Part of the court's justification for using teacher per-pupil costs was the belief that experience was related to teacher quality and that teacher costs were dependent on a pay scale that rewarded seniority. In his summary of the case, Horowitz did not find this assumption substantiated by research literature. For instance, after looking at the studies cited by the economists for the plaintiffs, Horowitz found research to support the idea that verbal scores on standardized tests are better predictors of student performance than experience. In addition, hiring teachers with higher verbal scores is less expensive than hiring teachers according to experience. Teacher experience, according to the research explored by Horowitz, helped the achievement scores of white students but not black students.

In his criticism of the court's use of social science data, Horowitz argues that if research is to be believed, then the court's remedy could not promote equality of achievement between black and white students. In addition, he states, the problem is even more fundamental. The available research on the relationship between costs and student achievement, Horowitz claims, is not substantial enough to draw any meaningful conclusions about the effect of finacial changes on equality of educational opportunity. In other words, the research in this area of education is not complete enough to support legal remedies based on changes in educational expenditures as related to student achievement.

If one accepts Horowitz's argument, then the use of social science data in court proceedings can be criticized on a number of points. One criticism is that most social science data are open to dispute by other social scientists. Another criticism is the court's difficulty in deciding academic disputes. In addition, there is a problem with court remedies that have no support in social science data or for which the data is open to dispute. This means that court decisions can be based on disputed data and that the remedies for those decisions can be based on equally disputed data.

As mentioned in the *Otero* case, a major difference between judicial and normal political decision making is that politics depends on compromise and accommodation of conflicting interests, while judicial actions require judgments about evidence given in an adversarial relationship. Therefore, if a judicial decision is made on the basis of faulty evidence or is the result of poor judgment, then the consequences of the decision might not be related to court's intentions. Of course, the same situation can arise in a political struggle between different sets of interests in which one or more parties miscalculates the way of best achieving their interests. In the case of *Hobson v. Hansen*, the final court decision caused unexpected results.

After the court's decision, the school board, as it considered the political consequences of its actions, further narrowed the remedy. According to Horowitz, the school board had several options for achieving equality between schools in per-pupil teacher costs. It could have moved teachers by compulsory transfers, moved students by compulsory busing, or have done both by closing schools and changing school boundaries. Because it believed the measures were unpopular with the public, the board rejected changing school boundaries, closing schools, and mandatory busing of students. This left only the transferring of teachers; and, of course, union seniority rules discouraged the mass transfer of teachers. The school board therefore had to comply with the remedy by devising a scheme that minimized teacher transfers. It accomplished this by focusing adjustments on special-subject teachers. Whenever a school's per-pupil teacher costs were high or low according to systemwide standards, special-subject teachers could be added or removed. Administratively, the transfer of special-subject teachers was easier than transferring regular teachers.

In other words, the court's need to find a measurable remedy worked together with the political process of the school system to reduce the issue of equality of educational opportunity for black students in the Washington, D.C., school system to the transfer of special-subject teachers. The major effect was to make the special-subject program in the schools a function of per-pupil teacher costs in each school. In turn, the per-pupil teacher costs in each school were a function of student-teacher ratios and the seniority of the school's teachers. This meant that the special-subjects program in the school system did not operate according to the educational needs of the students, but according to student-teacher ratios and teacher seniority.

As a result of this strange turn of events, the final remedy had little effect on equality of educational opportunity between blacks and whites. In fact, the remedy might have had the opposite effect. In the early 1970s some primarily black, low-income schools in the district experienced a rapid decline in enrollment. This caused the virtual elimination of special-subjects programs at those schools. During the same period of time, a large white school located in a high-income neighborhood experienced an increase in students, which caused an expanded special-subjects program. In fact, the school, because of its lower per-pupil teacher costs resulting from an increased student-teacher ratio, received extra funds to hire a second music teacher to establish a school orchestra and a teacher to provide French instruction beginning in the third grade. In addition, other schools attended by children from high-income families maintained special-subjects programs through outside funding. In the end, this meant that the final decree in *Hobson v. Hansen* caused the closing of special-subjects programs in some black elementary schools.

Hobson v. Hansen, Horowitz argues, is a good example of the difficulty the judiciary faces in decreeing remedies for social problems. Not only must the courts deal with highly debatable social science data in making a decision and planning a remedy, but they often have little control over the actual process of implementation. In this case, the already narrowed remedy of equalizing per-pupil teacher costs was reduced by the political process of the school system to the transferring of special-subject teachers. Therefore, the problem is not only with the judicial process, but with the political forces outside the judiciary that affect the implementation of judicial remedies.

CONCLUSION

Analyzing judicial involvement in educational policy making requires consideration of the following:

1. The representativeness of the individual or group initiating court action;
2. The type of evidence presented by plaintiffs and defendants;
3. The ability of the judge and lawyers to understand and use evidence based on social science data;
4. The relationship between the original complaint, the goals of the judge, and the court's remedy;
5. The effect of political forces outside of the court on the implementation of the court's remedy;
6. The actual results of the implementation of the court's decree.

Otero and *Hobson* provide good examples of issues surrounding representation and the capabilities of the courts to deal with educational issues. And *Hobson* shows what an impact court decisions can have on educational policies. In *Hobson*, the court's decree affected the budget, teacher transfers, and the curriculum in special-subject areas.

In general, court decisions touch a broad range of policy issues. In some situations, court decisions directly affect the political process by requiring election, as a means of assuring minority group representation, to local school boards by district, as opposed to at-large, elections.[26] In New Jersey, the actions of the state supreme court in trying to assure equality of educational spending resulted in the creation of a whole new layer of state bureaucracy to monitor compliance. In this situation, one result of court action was a change in the state educational bureaucracy.[27] Also, in most cases dealing with inequality of educational funding, the result is a change in state financing methods.[28]

Desegregation cases have affected the curriculum, school assignments, teacher transfers, administrative organization, tracking, ability grouping, and transportation.[29] Cases brought by religious groups have affected religious practices in schools, textbooks, the curriculum, and state laws.[30] Free-speech issues have involved the courts in methods of book selection and in the treatment of students and teachers by school systems. Due process requirements have formalized the relationship between students, teachers, and administrative staff.[31]

There is practically no area of educational policy making that has not been touched by court action. Primarily, judicial action has been taken to protect religious and free-speech rights under the First Amendment, and equal-protection and due process rights under the Fourteenth Amendment. The major problem faced by the courts in the protection of these rights is the introduction of evidence based on the often confusing and contradictory results of educational research, and the implementation of decisions in the complicated arena of the educational politics.

NOTES

1. *Wisconsin v. Yoder*, 406 U.S. 205 (1972).
2. Brown v. Board of Education of Topeka, 347 U.S. 483 (1954).
3. *Pennsylvania Association for Retarded Children v. Commonwealth of Pennsylvania*, 343 F. Supp. 279 (E.D. Pa 1972); and *Lau v. Nichols*, 414 U.S. 563 (1974).
4. Tom Mirga, "On Trial—'Secular Humanism' in Schools: Federal Judge Considers Arguments in Alabama," *Education Week*, Vol. 6, No. 6 (October 15, 1986), 1, 13, 18.
5. Deborah L. Rhode, "Conflicts of Interest in Educational Reform Litigation," In David Kirp and Donald Jensen, eds., *School Days, Rule Days: The Legalization and Regulation of Education* (Philadelphia: Falmer Press, 1986), pp. 278–302.
6. Michael Rebell and Arthur Block, *Educational Policy Making and the Courts* (Chicago: University of Chicago Press, 1982), pp. 11–14.
7. Ibid., pp. 14–15; and Lino A. Graglia, *Disaster by Decree: The Supreme Court*

Decisions on Race and the Schools (Ithaca, N.Y.: Cornell University Press, 1976).

8. *Ingraham v. Wright*, 430 U.S. 651 (1977).
9. *West Virginia State Board of Education v. Barnette*, 319 U.S. 624 (1943).
10. Albert Keim, ed., *Compulsory Education and the Amish* (Boston: Beacon Press, 1972).
11. *State of Wisconsin, Petitioner v. Jonas Yoder et al.*, 406 U.S. 205 (1972).
12. *Engel v. Vitale*, 370 U.S. 421 (1962).
13. *Tinker v. Des Moines Independent Community School District*, 393 U.S. 503 (1969).
14. *Goss v. Lopez*, 419 U.S. 565, 581 (1975).
15. *Brown v. Board of Education of Topeka*, 347 U.S. 482 (1954).
16. *Lau v. Nichols*, 414 U.S. 563 (1974).
17. *San Antonio Independent School District v. Rodriquez*, 411 U.S. 1 (1973).
18. Rebell and Block, *Educational Policy Making*, pp. 123–47.
19. Ibid., p. 43.
20. Ibid., p. 215.
21. Ibid., p. 164.
22. Donald L. Horowitz, *The Courts and Social Policy* (Washington, D.C.: Brookings Institute, 1977), p. 281.
23. Ibid., p. 264.
24. Ibid., pp. 106–70.
25. Ibid., p. 133.
26. See *Sierra v. El Paso Independent School District*, 591 F. Supp. 802 (W.D. Texas 1984).
27. R. Lehne, *The Quest for Justice: The Politics of School Finance Reform* (White Plains, N.Y.: Longman, 1978).
28. R. Elmore and M. McLaughlin, *Reform and Retrenchment: The Politics of School Finance Reform* (Cambridge, Mass.: Ballinger, Inc., 1982).
29. R. L. Crain et al. *The Politics of School Desegregation* (Chicago: Aldine, 1968).
30. Keim, Albert, ed., *Compulsory Education and the Amish*.
31. For coverage of legal issues affecting teachers and students, see Louis Fischer, David Schimmel, and Cynthia Kelly, *Teachers and the Law* (White Plains, N.Y.: Longman, 1987).

CHAPTER 8

The Political Control of Education in a Democratic Society

The central issue regarding the political control of education is who should decide what knowledge is of most worth. In general, American educational theorists have avoided this issue because it questions the legitimacy of their attempts to impose educational change on American schools. Obviously, they do not want to deal with this problem when they think they have all the answers on how to improve the public schools. Most often, these theorists are more interested in questions of implementation than of who should have the power to decide what is best. In addition, interest groups want a political organization under which the public schools serve their needs.

In this chapter we shall identify the main problems in the political control of education. We assume that there is a relationship between the political control of schooling and the political education of students. In other words, how the schools are controlled determines the content of learning, which in turn affects the political education of future citizens. More simply stated, the political control of schooling determines the political content of schooling.

The major problems in the political control of American schools are conflicts between free access to knowledge and majoritarian control, and the attempt by special-interest groups to make public schools serve their needs. Both situations involve attempts to control the content of knowledge in the public schools.

THE PROBLEM OF MAJORITARIAN CONTROL

Under majoritarian control, a majority of the people determines what knowledge is of most worth. Of course, this democratic determination of the content of schooling severely limits the types of knowledge taught in the schools. In particular, minority viewpoints regarding politics, culture, and social organization are excluded from the curriculum. Thus the parameters of political dialogue are narrowed, and political learning is reduced to consensus values.

Rather than being arenas for the free exchange of political ideas, the public schools become institutions for the imposition of values and ideas that are inoffensive to most of the people. This is precisely the outcome that was predicted by the father of the American common school, Horace Mann. He argued that political controversy, including controversial ideas, had to be excluded from common schools because including it would cause warring public factions to destroy the schools.[1]

Ironically, therefore, democratic, or majoritarian, control of the public schools limits the free political dialogue that some people argue is necessary for the maintenance of a democratic society. This argument assumes that the free exchange of ideas and a wide-ranging political dialogue are necessary for a dynamic and truly participatory democratic system. Thus, the democratic control of public schools could be said to contain the seeds of destruction of a democratic society.

On the other hand, some people argue that the limitation of political dialogue by democratically controlled schools creates political and social stability. From this perspective, narrowing the parameters of political dialogue reduces the possibility of political conflict. Some people argue that this places necessary curbs on the potential for democratic societies to create excessive political activity.

Concepts of citizenship are sharply divided between those who believe that a wide-ranging political dialogue is necessary for maintaining a democratic society and those who believe that limiting such dialogue is essential for political stability. One side wants the schools to produce active citizens who have the intellectual tools to participate in democratic control. The other side wants citizens who are educated to obey the law and assume the responsibilities of government. One group emphasizes an active concept of citizenship, the other a passive concept.

While the majoritarian control of public schools suggests a conflict between the democratic control of education and the preparation for democratic citizenship, our analysis of how American schools are actually controlled, as given in the previous chapters, presents a different set of issues. In reality, the public school system is a battleground for groups seeking to have knowledge used in their interests.

Of primary importance are the continual attempts by business interests to shape the schools to meet their economic needs. The period of the 1980s has seen business interests assuming ever-greater control of state education policies, local school districts signing compacts with private industry councils, and corporations participating in adopt-a-school programs. The pattern represents a continuation of the human capital theories that fostered the rise of vocational education in the early part of the twentieth century. Since then, the educational goal of preparing citizens for participation in a democracy has been replaced by that of preparing them for employment.

In keeping with an economic system based on the pursuit of profit, business interests are primarily concerned that public schools serve their needs. But business groups are often preoccupied with short-range goals, and one of their overriding concerns is to reduce employment costs in order to increase profits. Therefore, while the preparation of all students for employment is a laudable ideal, schools have a difficult time achieving this objective because of the influence of business.

In the first place, the short-range economic goals of business are responsible for the constant changes in educational policies. One needs only to contrast the major goals of schooling in the 1970s with those of the 1980s. The career and vocational education thrust of the public schools of the 1970s was replaced in the 1980s by the demands of business interests for more scientists and engineers. In fact, the business goals of the 1980s were similar to those of the 1950s, when it was considered necessary to have more scientists and engineers in order to win the technological race with the Soviet Union.

These constant changes in economic goals make it difficult to predict future job markets and are a reflection of the fact that business groups are primarily interested in meeting short-range needs. Except for gross predictions regarding the numbers of workers entering the labor market, economists cannot predict accurately the shape of future labor markets. Unexpected events upset economic predictions. The Vietnam war in the 1960s, the energy crisis of the 1970s, and international competition in the 1980s are some of the unforeseen factors that have shaped the American labor market. It would have been difficult for economists to have predicted these events and included them in long-range economic forecasting.

Therefore, educational goals based on projected economic needs could actually have a negative impact on students. Consider a situation that might have occurred for many students in the late 1950s and early 1960s: A student enters the first grade at a time when business is proclaiming a shortage of scientists and engineers. The student remains in school, including college, for approximately sixteen years.

However, economic conditions change dramatically during this time. The student graduates from college in 1971, near the end of the Vietnam War and the beginning of the energy crisis, just when demand for scientists and engineers is at its lowest. Consequently, the student cannot find a job.[2]

Not only can a student's future career be damaged by educational goals based on the predicted needs of the labor market, but also by the desire of business interests to reduce labor costs. If labor costs follow the law of supply and demand, then business has to be interested in maintaining a large labor supply as a means of keeping wages and salaries down. In fact, business is in the most advantageous position, with regard to labor costs, when there is an oversupply of workers in needed job categories.

When business interests claim, therefore, that there is a shortage of trained workers in a particular job category, it may be because they are being forced to pay higher salaries. In other words, business interests, feeling the impact of increasing wage costs, might declare a shortage of workers in order to ultimately reduce those costs. The public schools will then respond by training more workers, and the labor market will be flooded with workers trained for that particular job category, which, in turn, will cause salaries and labor costs to decrease.

While it is difficult to determine to what degree the declared shortage of scientists and engineers in the 1950s and 1980s was the result of business feeling the pressure of increased labor costs, one could hypothesize the following scenario. In the 1950s, business interests, in reaction to increasing costs for engineers and scientists, put pressure on the schools to increase training in those areas. As a result, the labor market was flooded with scientists and engineers by the late 1960s, which drove down salaries and labor costs. Consequently, business stopped pressuring the schools for training in those areas; and, because of reduced salaries and employment problems, fewer students chose to enter those fields. As a result by the early 1980s the supply of engineers and scientists was low; and business, beginning to experience rising labor costs in those areas, began again to pressure the schools to emphasize science and mathematics.

Business's concern with lowering labor costs can also be found at the local level. Consider the example of magnet schools in Atlanta, where advisory boards provide "continual counsel so that the curriculum and its delivery stay attuned to developments within the industry." Two of the magnet schools, the Harper Center for Financial Services and the Roosevelt Center for Information Processing and Decision Making, directly serve the needs of local business. In particular, the Harper Center for Financial Services is designed to provide workers for the local banking industry and has on its advisory board representatives from eight local banks, including the Federal Reserve.[3] In this situation, if the financial industry were to look out for its own interests, it would want the school to flood the labor market in order to lower labor costs and to provide it with the opportunity to pick the best graduates.

The influence of business interests on the public schools also raises the question of whether or not the public should pay the expenses of employment training. For instance, in the case of Atlanta's Harper Center for Financial Services, an argument can be made that business interests should pay all training expenses, since they are the primary beneficiaries. The public schools, at public expense, could provide a sound basic education, and business, at business's expense, could provide the job training. If business assumed all costs of training, rather than the public schools at public expense, there would be less temptation to flood the labor market with graduates trained in particular skills. As long as business interests can pressure public schools to serve their needs, then public schools will be used to ensure increased private profits at public expense.

Of course, business is not the only interest group seeking to have the schools serve its needs. Private foundations and single-interest groups try to influence the schools to serve their particular ideologies. Teachers' and administrators' associations work for policies that will serve their interests, but not necessarily those of students.

As described in Chapter 1, the result of pressures from various interest groups, elected politicians, and educational politicians is an education system in a constant state of change. Such continual change creates unknown costs that never seem justified by the results. Education, despite endless new programs, has not eliminated poverty, solved problems of national defense, ended unemployment, or resolved any of the other social problems foisted on the schools. Some might argue that because of the constant state of change, the schools never have sufficient time to solve any one economic or social problem. The goals of the system change so swiftly that nothing is ever given a chance to work. On the other hand, it could be argued that schools cannot solve major social and economic problems. From this perspective, it is not that the schools fail, but that they truly do not have the power to reform society and save the economic system.

Measuring the economic costs of change in education is a complex job. At the federal level, one has to consider the actual costs of developing and implementing new programs, along with the money spent on the programs themselves. The same is true at the state and local levels. Each change in national and state educational goals breeds a new crop of administrators in state departments of education and the central offices of local school systems. And, as we have seen, these administrators form their own interest groups to fight for more funding.

In addition, there are the costs of financing the research programs that usually accompany each new direction in national and state education policies. One cost is the funding of the great army of educational researchers that inhabit colleges of education around the country and whose professional lives depend on each swing of the policy pendulum. It would certainly be interesting to do a cost-effectiveness study to see whether or not educational research has improved student learning. For intance, has all the money spent on reading research since the 1950s produced any improvement in students' reading skills?

Educators are often the last to admit that schools cannot solve the world's problems. It is in their interest to accept and promote the idea of schooling as a panacea for society's problems. By promoting the school as an instrument of economic and social reform, public-school people can demand more financial support. The idea of education as a social panacea also increases public-school professionals' feelings of self-worth.

POLITICAL STRUCTURE AND METHODS OF INSTRUCTION

As a result of outside pressure, and the willingness and necessity of public-school people to respond to that pressure, students are viewed as products to be managed for the good of those who have the greatest influence on the schools. In other words, as a result of the control by interest groups, the primary institutional goal of public schooling becomes service to those interest groups. As a result, school administrators and teachers direct all their efforts toward educating students to meet the needs of outside interest groups.

The political structure of schooling thus has a profound effect on education methods. If public schools were concerned only with serving a consumer class of students, as opposed to outside interest groups and politicians, then instruction would be oriented toward serving the desires of students and parents. In other words, methods of instruction vary according to whether schools are oriented to serving outside interests or consumers. When they must serve outside interests, school administrators and teachers become preoccupied with methods of managing student behavior and learning, and not with satisfying consumer needs.

Consider the following hypothesis regarding instructional methods in American public schools. Given a variety of psychological theories and methods of instruction, public schools, serving outside interests, tend to choose those theories and methods that emphasize the management of student behavior and learning. This desire to manage learning and behavior to serve outside interest groups and politicians thus determines what instructional methods the public schools adopt.

One can contrast instruction methods based on behavioral psychology with those proposed by John Dewey. The reason behavioral psychology has had such a great impact on American classrooms, as opposed to Dewey's theories, is that it emphasizes the control and management of student behavior to achieve specific objectives. On the other hand, John Dewey's pedagogy emphasizes instruction that is based on student interests, on giving students the intellectual tools to direct their own learning, and on educating students to participate in the shaping of economic and political institutions. Dewey's pedagogy can be considered to be consumer-oriented because it enhances the power of students to control their own lives. Behavioral psychology, on the other hand, allows institutions to manage and control student learning for objectives established by the political forces that control the schools.

Particular psychological theories are used in education because they serve certain purposes. Because a variety of competing psychological theories exists and there is no agreement about which theory best describes human behavior, an institution like the public school system can choose a theory that serves its institutional purposes. In other words, lacking any agreed-upon truth about human behavior, the choice of psychological methods to apply in the schools is a political decision.

The major competing theories of instruction in United States in the twentieth century are those of John Dewey, and behavioral psychologists like Edward Thorndike and B. F. Skinner. Of course, there has also been a stream of developmental theory from G. Stanley Hall to Piaget. If one were to rank-order the impact of these three psychological perspectives on American education in the twentieth century, one would see that behaviorism has had the greatest impact, followed by the developmentalists, with John Dewey having the least influence of the three. This order of influence has occurred not because one theory is more accurate than another, but because of political decisions. Consider the changes in emphasis in psychological theories in the schools from the 1970s to the 1980s. In the 1970s, one of the primary objectives of the conservative reaction to campus protests against the Vietnam War, urban violence, and the growing use of drugs was the restoration of law and order. This meant the management and control of student behavior, and a curriculum emphasis on career and vocational education. The dominant methods of instruction during this period were competency-based education and teaching by specific behavioral objectives. In addition, school administrators attempted to control teachers through management by behavioral objectives. During the 1970s, students in colleges of education, administrators in the public schools, and teachers in classrooms were asked to produce long lists of specific behavioral objectives that were to be achieved by modifying student behavior.[4]

In the 1980s, with the election of President Reagan, the educational constituency of the Republican party demanded a restoration of morality in the public schools, and the business community demanded higher academic standards in order to win the international trade war with Japan and West Germany. Most often, these two objectives were brought together, as was the case with Secretary of Education William Bennett and California's Superintendent of Instruction Bill Honig, in the advocacy of a strong academic curriculum that would teach moral values.

Paralleling these shifts in educational goals were changes in the application of psychological theory to the management of students and teachers. Rather than being concerned with the control of outward behavior through management and teaching by behavioral objectives, cognitive psychology and metacognition focused on the decision making and learning strategies of students and teachers. Research in the 1980s suggested that because of the constantly changing conditions of classroom life, teachers found it almost impossible to follow a lesson plan based on specific behavioral objectives. In fact, it was argued, the best yardstick for measuring teacher performance was the ability to make good decisions in a continually changing classroom environment. Thus the most important thing was to train teachers to make good decisions. A similar argument was made regarding student learning. The key to learning was not to reward proper behavior, but to have students make decisions about correct learning strategies.[5]

These changes in the management of teachers and students were directly related to the moral emphasis given to the academic curriculum in the 1980s. Rather than control future behavior through behavior modification, the emphasis in the 1980s has been to control future moral actions by schooling children to make correct moral decisions. The proposals for a core curriculum have now been designed to provide the content of moral judgment, while instructional methods based on cognitive and metacognitive psychology have been designed to ensure that good decisions will be made with the moral content. In other words, in the 1980s concern with controlling the outward behavior of students has been replaced with concerns with controlling the thinking processes of students.

Admittedly, the above argument regarding such changes between the 1970s and 1980s is a hypothesis, but it does illustrate how the political structure of schooling can determine the methods of instruction. The control of public schools by special-interest groups and politicians has produced instructional methods that manage student learning in order to achieve a constantly changing set of educational goals. Instructional methods that are based on student interests and that give students the power to direct their own learning require a school system that is not politically structured to serve the needs of interest groups and the policy goals of government.

Therefore, the present political structure of public schooling in the United States results in an education that is antithetical to the idea of active, self-directed democratic citizens. Majoritarian control, when it occurs, reduces the parameters of political learning and dialogue in the schools, and makes political education into the teaching of consensus values and the training in a passive form of citizenship. Control by interest groups results in educational goals that serve the needs of those interest groups, and an educational system in a constant state of change.

The political structure of schooling determines the political content of education and the methods of instruction. As long as the public schools in the United States are controlled by a majority or by special-interest groups, students will be educated for passive democratic citizenship. If the school system is going to prepare active democratic citizens, the political control of American education will have to be restructured.

THE CONTROL OF SCHOOLING IN A DEMOCRATIC SOCIETY

There has never been a major discussion of the relationship between the political control of knowledge and republican and democratic forms of government. Consequently, the American school system has developed without any vision of its ultimate political organization. The beliefs and power struggles of each historical period have influenced the way in which local and state governments have organized schools systems and teacher-training institutions, passed certification laws, and established standards and goals. Certainly, few people in the nineteenth century could have predicted that in the twentieth century the federal government would play a major role in shaping educational policy to ensure the protection of civil rights, or that schools would be enlisted in an international cold war or a domestic war on poverty.

The topsy-turvy development of American schools has occurred with only minor debates about the ideal political structure for an educational system in a democratic society. Some ideals of control have been mentioned in passing, but without any serious attention to their implications for democratic ideals in education. Frequently, people will speak of the value of "local control" while forgetting that local control in the past often brought about school systems that were segregated, that discriminated against the poor, and that primarily served the interests of local elites. It should not be forgotten that the campaign for equality of educational opportunity was not championed by local school systems, but by the courts and the federal government. And this occurred only after the groups who had been receiving such unequal treatment realized that local control did not work in their interests and that they would have to seek redress from other branches of government.

As discussed in Chapter 5, local control usually means control by local boards of education, which, given the nature of election laws and local power structures, are either dominated by local elites or are torn apart by factional disputes. One alternative to this traditional model of local control is community control of schools, in which all local citizens have an opportunity to participate directly in decisions about curriculum, teacher hiring, textbook selection, budgets, and the whole range of school activities. But this alternative brings with it the problems of majoritarian control.

One alternative to local and community control is to place the control of schooling in the hands of educational professionals. Using the slogan, "Take the Schools out of Politics," educational reformers in the early part of the twentieth century tried to turn over the control of public schools to educational experts. Rather than taking the schools out of politics, this reform added the dimension of administrative politics. As we have pointed out, educational bureaucrats pursue power and income, and they are often in conflict with organized teachers' groups. And, of course, there are constant complaints about the functioning of school bureaucracies.

The alternative between the two extremes of community control and professional control is the establishment of school advisory groups that are representative of the local community. Ideally, these advisory groups would work with school administrators in deciding school policies. The problem with this approach, however, is that decision making at the school level, and indeed at the community level, is really marginal to the power of state and federal governments.

This line of reasoning brings us back to the problem of the constantly shifting nature of state and federal educational policies. In addition, educators and politicians have not adequately discussed what kind of relationship between local, state, and federal governments would be best in the formulation of educational policy. The major exception, as discussed in Chapter 3, was the effort by the Reagan administration in the early 1980s to deregulate and reduce federal control through block grant programs. But even in this instance, there never was a full-scale debate on an optimum political structure for American education.

A Fourth Branch of Government

Before things become any more complex, it is necessary to begin considering the best means of governing an educational system in a democratic society. The following proposal is given with a minimum of detail about how it would actually function; obviously, it will need to be altered and refined.

The proposal is premised on several beliefs. The first is that one of the most important aspects of a democratic society is freedom of ideas. As we have seen, political pressures and value conflicts do not promote the free expression of ideas in public schools. In the United States, there is greater freedom of expression in books in privately owned book stores than there is in the public schools. This is an amazing situation, considering the rhetoric one hears about the importance of schooling for a democratic society. A major problem in the democratic control of schools is that value conflicts most often prevent controversial ideas from being presented in the public schools.

Second, a major political issue in American education is the ability of groups to use the public schools to promote their own special interests. In the twentieth century, business groups have had an enormous influence on the public schools. Other private groups have been able to gain control of public institutions and have them serve their needs.

American schools have also been harmed by being made the dumping ground for a broad array of social problems. Politicians and special-interest groups have often found the public schools to be a convenient, uncontroversial place for initiating solutions to problems ranging from traffic accidents to AIDS. Moreover, educators seldom say No to an offer of more money, even if they know the schools cannot do the job.

Given this framework, the problem is to create a political structure for education that can maintain freedom of ideas, minimize the influence of special-interest groups, and reduce the use of the schools for solving social problems. One possible solution is to make public schooling, through a constitutional amendment, the fourth branch of government with the same protection from outside influences that is given to the Supreme Court and the Federal Reserve Bank.

Obviously, no branch of government can be completely free of outside influences. The Supreme Court has been politicized by the process by which its members are appointed. The administration in power fills vacant seats on the Supreme Court with justices attuned to the administration's political philosophy. The same is true of the Federal Reserve.

While complete freedom from outside influences is impossible, a structure could be created that would minimize the influence of special-interest groups. In addition, this new branch of government would be organized to protect and support the free expression of ideas.

To accomplish the above, control of the fourth branch of government should be given to a board of teachers, who would be appointed for life by members of the teaching profession. Any person who had a teaching certificate would be eligible to vote and would be a candidate for the controlling board. National teaching certificates would be issued by this new educational branch of government.

The fourth branch of government would call meetings of a national assembly of teachers elected by fellow teachers to determine teacher certification requirements, teacher education requirements, academic requirements for schools, and national educational policy. All public schools would be controlled by this branch of government. The assembly of teachers would decide the degree of flexibility to be given to each teacher and local school system.

The major ideal of this branch of government would be to protect the free exchange and transmission of ideas. It is assumed that ideas receive maximum support when they are linked to self-interest. In this situation, the protection of the freedom of ideas justifies the existence of a separate educational branch of government and professional autonomy. Therefore, under these conditions the teaching profession would champion the ideal of the free exchange and transmission of ideas out of regard for its own self-interest.

If it is assumed that teachers will pursue their own interests, then funding should be controlled by Congress. Otherwise, teachers in this branch of government would appropriate an endless amount of money for the schools. The amendment to the Constitution that would establish education as the fourth branch of government should also include a provision for Congress to allocate general, and not categorical funding for education.

Letting the Consumer Choose

Another alternative to establishing a fourth branch of government is to give control to consumers through a voucher or tuition tax credit plan. Theoretically, this would require schools to respond to consumer demands regarding curriculum contact and methods of instruction. Giving money for education directly to the consumer in the form of a voucher or tax credit might shift the locus of control. The word "might" is used because state regulation of schools might continue government control over the curriculum. In other words, special-interest groups working through the regulatory function of government could limit the amount of choice by prescribing general goals for the curriculum, mandating state tests, and selecting textbooks. For a choice system to contribute to meaningful diversity in education, state regulation of schools would have to be eliminated or limited to health and safety issues.

A potential problem with a choice system is that the educational system might be dominated by the profit motive. Schools might be concerned primarily with cost-effectiveness, as opposed to diversity of content and methods. The orientation might be toward selling a product through good packaging, advertising, and promotion. The student might be treated as a product that would have to be efficiently managed to decrease costs (in many respects, this is similar to the treatment under the current structure of schooling). The goal of cost-effectiveness might emphasize student performance on standardized tests as opposed to empowering students with the knowledge and abilities by which they could guide their own destinies.

Indeed, a choice system could lead to the ownership of schools by large corporations. It is not difficult to imagine IBM marketing a series of educational institutions in the same manner that hamburgers are currently sold. If this were to occur, then education would be dominated even more by business interests than it now is.

Proposals for education as a fourth branch of government and a choice system involve a radical restructuring of the politics of American education. These proposals provide a beginning for a national dialogue about the political structure of American education. So far, in the history of education, there has been no extensive debate about the appropriate political structure for education in a democratic and free society. As stated previously, the political structure of schooling determines its political content and methods of instruction. And if the political content of schooling and methods of intruction affect students, then the political structure of schooling affects the type of citizen produced by the public schools. In other words, the politics of education has a determining influence on the quality and nature of American life.

NOTES

1. For a discussion of this political dilemma, see Joel Spring, *The American School: 1642–1985* (White Plains, N.Y.: Longman, 1986), pp. 80–90.
2. For a discussion of the problems of linking schooling with labor market needs, see Richard Freeman, *The Overeducated American* (New York: Academic Press, 1976).
3. Kathryn Borman and Joel Spring, *Schools in Central Cities* (White Plains, N.Y.: Longman, 1984), p. 182.
4. For a study of the conservative reaction of the 1970s, see Ira Shore, *Culture Wars: School and Soceity in the Conservative Restoration, 1969–1984* (Boston: Routledge & Kegan Paul, 1986).
5. For a review of research on teaching in the 1980s, see Lee Shulman, "Paradigms and Research Programs in the Study of Teaching: A Contemporary Perspective," in Merlin Wittrock, ed., *Handbook of Research on Teaching*, 3rd ed. (New York: Macmillian, 1986).

Index